STARS BENEATH US

STARS BENEATH US

FINDING GOD IN THE EVOLVING COSMOS

PAUL WALLACE

Fortress Press

Minneapolis

STARS BENEATH US
Finding God in the Evolving Cosmos

Cover design: Brad Norr

Library of Congress Cataloging-in-Publication Data
Print ISBN: 978-1-5064-0141-6
eBook ISBN: 978-1-5064-0142-3

The paper used in this publication meets the minimum requirements of American
National Standard for Information Sciences — Permanence of Paper for Printed
Library Materials, ANSI Z329.48-1984.

Manufactured in the U.S.A.

Contents

INTRODUCTION

One of the finest things about teaching is being present for exact moments of understanding. You can't always be there when these happen, and, strictly speaking, you can't always know it when they do. But when lights turn on they can be hard to hide, especially if they're of the high-wattage variety.

The most memorable moment of this kind happened for me about ten years ago. It was the first day of one of my introductory astronomy classes. Such courses often begin with the obvious view, the night sky as seen with the unaided eye, and this one was no exception. As part of my standard opening spiel I mentioned this modest fact: Under a dark and transparent atmosphere, with an unobstructed horizon and healthy vision, one can see at most about 3,000 stars. And if we were to remove our home planet from under our feet we would see 3,000 more, for a total of 6,000 stars. In general students are mildly surprised that the number is so small—some expect millions. We chatted about it briefly. Then I glanced down at my notes and prepared to move on to the next topic, the constellations.

When I looked up I was surprised to see an expression of near-trauma spread across a student's face. I will never forget it. He was sitting on the left, two rows back, scarcely breathing. It was so surprising that I paused and asked him if he was okay. Was it something I said?

His look of horror turned into a sheepish grin and he explained himself: "It's just that you said that there are stars under my feet, and I had never really thought of it like that before. Wow!"

Then, to everyone's delight, he laughed out loud.

He was about twenty years old and a very good student. Was he really learning this for the first time? Could he have possibly missed something so obvious?

It's unlikely. I suspect something more interesting happened that day. He had known the fact for years: The spherical Earth is surrounded on all sides by stars. But until that day this knowledge was a mere concept for him, like a dry husk encasing a bud of green actuality. At the moment in question the husk fell away and reality was recovered. The stricken look on his face suggested to me that the stars far beneath his seat became tangible to him in that instant, that the words *up* and *down* momentarily lost all content. Perhaps he felt the faint flutter of vertigo. He certainly felt *something*. In that short span of time the absolute became relative and the strangeness of the world was revealed in all its simplicity.

We are not accustomed to finding ourselves within the cosmos we imagine. We know that the Earth and other planets go around the Sun, but it is a strange and wonderful experience to lie under the night sky, locate two or three planets, and use them to get a physical sense of the solar system, to see and to *feel* its actual tilt and turn, and to find yourself in it. It's fun to familiarize yourself with the basics of evolution, but deeply mysterious to locate your own tiny and particular self within its great stream. Chemistry is interesting on a blackboard, but mind-blowing when you become aware of it working within your own body, silently keeping you alive moment by moment.

I have read many books, academic and popular, on the well-worn topic of religion-and-science. I have attended (and delivered) more than my share of religion-and-science lectures and watched more than my share of religion-and-science debates. I have taught religion-and-science courses in churches, colleges, and seminaries. These experiences have taught me a lot about the topic and about the great interest many people have in it. They have also led me to conclude that, at the popular level, the topic has become as lifeless as a husk.

You may disagree. The Internet is full of people arguing about this issue; books about religion and science tend to sell; religion-versus-science debates make for exceedingly popular viewing; evolution continues to divide Christians in America. How can I claim this topic is lifeless? How is it dull? Because the issue has stagnated. People are arguing and books are selling, but (again, at the popular level) I have not encountered a new argument or sensed any development since at least 1999, well before Richard Dawkins and his fellow New Atheists revved up their scientifically motivated harangue against religion of all kinds (what's new about them is their attitude, not their arguments).[1] There is plenty of noise but no life. Nothing new is happening.

The popular media tend to emphasize the divide between those who embrace science and reject all forms of religion (e.g., the New Atheists) and those who embrace religion and reject science (e.g., creationists). These two groups seem to do little more than heave rhetorical bombs at one another. Such bombast sells books, and there's nothing like it for fueling Internet rage, but man is it *boring*.

Between these extremes is a broad field occupied by those who wish to reconcile religion and science. In general they believe, as I do, that there is no essential conflict between the religious and the scientific. Many in the middle have labored honorably to bring these

---

1. 1999 is the year that Kenneth Miller's *Finding Darwin's God* was published. It contains what I believe is a novel discussion—which I ultimately find unsatisfying—about God's action in the world.

two great ways of knowing together, and, seeing how neither religion nor science seems to be going anywhere soon, I believe the future belongs to them. I value their erudition and their dedication to the hard work of peacemaking.

But frankly, I find nearly all of the (popular) middle-ground work to be unconvincing. Much of it is written by traditional Christians who love and understand science, but who nevertheless tend to view science as a problem that must somehow be "dealt with" or worked around by people of faith. They never allow science or the cosmos to shape their theology at a deep level. The driving idea behind much of their work seems to be that if you're creative and put in enough effort, you can bring traditional Christianity together with the evolving cosmos in such a way that both retain their integrity. And they may even succeed at this, at least in the narrow sense of logical consistency. The academic problem may be solved, but the resulting models are so out of harmony with themselves, so unwieldy, monstrous, oftentimes goofy, and so contrary to lived experience that it seems hardly worth the effort.[2]

This must be a result of the relentlessly academic nature of the topic. There seems to be a widespread belief that religion-and-science is, at root, an intellectual issue and therefore it must be explored by purely intellectual methods. This is an understandable mistake, for religion-and-science writers must import ideas from (at least) the fields of science, theology, and philosophy. Each of these is a vast discipline—or, to be precise, family of disciplines—with its own language, assumptions, and values. When you bring them together in an attempt to construct a universal model of reality, it can bog down into a head game pretty quickly. Unwieldy, monstrous, and goofy results come as no surprise at all.

---

2. The unmanageability of the topic is evidenced by its very name: religion-and-science. There really should be a single word for it.

One solution to this problem is to start not with universal principles or concepts but with normal human life. A wise pastor friend once advised me that, whenever an issue is to be worked out, you should do what Jesus did: "Start with the person." At the time we were talking about same-sex marriage, but I think his suggestion can be applied to religion-and-science. *Stars Beneath Us* is, so far as I know, the first religion-and-science book written from a consistently—and explicitly—personal perspective.

The personal is what moves us. The personal is what changes us and might even open us to the world. Concepts alone have little power for deep change; they must be rooted in life as we know it. When they do connect, when one's ideas and one's actual life are woven together, great things start happening. Just ask that student in my class. It was not his head knowledge alone that shocked him that day. He had known the facts since he was a child. But at that moment, what had for years been merely conceptual became, to use a stained-glass word, incarnational. The facts never went away, but they became profoundly present in such a way that he himself got involved. He was no longer playing with an idea; he was being played by reality. The stars were not just in his head; they were actually and truly *down there*, light years beneath his sneakers.

This book has been a long time coming, and I'm grateful to Tony Jones for seeing something good in my proposal and for believing it could work. Thanks go out to him and to Lisa Gruenisen for seeing it through to completion. To those behind the scenes at Fortress who made the book possible, thank you. I am also grateful to my dear friend Jake Myers who connected me with Fortress in the first place.

There is nothing new under the sun, and I must mention two people whose work has deeply affected me and who will see their influence in *Stars Beneath Us*. Catherine Keller, whose *Face of the Deep* almost single-handedly shook me out of my fixation on classical theism and simultaneously alerted me to the bottomless riches of the book of Job, is one of them. Reading her work is like walking into the studio of a great artist: her intelligence is matched only by her creativity and imagination. William Brown made me love Job even more with his brilliant *Seven Pillars of Creation*. I am grateful to him not only for that outstanding book but for his friendship.

My brother-in-law Keith Pierce is not an editor, but he should be. He faithfully read through every chapter as I wrote them and went over every last word of the final manuscript. His sharp eye, his experience as a reader, and his sensitivity to language and his knowledge of "how books should go" made him an invaluable help throughout the writing process. I also thank my friend Ben Reiss, who encouraged me to keep sending off book proposals when I had nearly surrendered my dream of being an author.

Mark Sargent's honest words from the pulpit of Rome First United Methodist Church set me on the path that led to my ordination and to this book, and I will always be grateful for his presence on this planet. I am indebted to Greg Lovell and Michael Tutterow for keeping me on that path when night fell and I couldn't see a thing, not even the stars.

To my people at Agnes Scott College: thank you for supporting me in my rather unconventional career. To my people at Berry College, particularly Michael Bailey, Ron Taylor, and Todd Timberlake: thank you for not disowning me when I left. To my people at First Baptist Church of Decatur: thank you for letting me off the deacon and Sunday-school-teaching hooks while I worked on this book. I'm coming back now.

My family knows how long and strange the road has been, and if they hadn't been on it with me I would have given up long ago. I thank all of them to the moon and back: Dad, Mom, Mom, Dan, Kristen, Sherry, Keith, and all the cousins. My aunt Bettie Clark's interest in me and support of my work have made this book possible. To her I send profound gratitude. My children Henry, Julia, and

Kristen probably don't know what an education and inspiration they have been to me, but I've never learned so much or laughed so much as I have with them. Where do such beautiful people come from?

Finally, as Johnny Cash says, I've got a woman who knows her man. Elizabeth has been my partner in marriage for nearly twenty-five years, and with her help I've come to know the beauty and miraculous love this human life offers, and to accept it. *Stars Beneath Us* is dedicated to her.

 CHAPTER 1

IS THIS WHAT LOVE LOOKS LIKE?

I was talking on the telephone in a dark room when I realized for the first time that Adam and Eve had not been actual people. I was twelve or thirteen. With one hand I held the receiver and with the other I spun the long helical cord like a jump rope, its far end lost in the light spilling in under the door to the kitchen. On the other side, activity and sound: Mom preparing supper, my siblings' voices. I suppose my presence was betrayed to them only by the to-and-fro motion of the cord under the door. Strangely, I don't remember the conversation or who was on the line. But as I stood there talking in the dark I just knew it: the First Couple were figurative.

It was a question I had been working on for a while. Not long before this, my dad had handed me a Time-Life book about natural history. It was one of a series that covered every imaginable scientific topic: meteorology, relativity, biochemistry, evolution. We had the whole set on the shelf above the stereo in the living room. The book in question featured a two-page, color-coded geologic timeline. By its lights, Dad and I located ourselves within the Holocene epoch of the Quaternary period of the Cenozoic era of the Phanerozoic eon, right up there at the top. We sat on the sofa and together peered down the well of deep time.

At its lowest and narrowest place lurked the Hadean Eon, marking Earth's assembly four-and-a-half billion years ago. Within a billion years, rudimentary life began to stir. From there on up the chart complexified like life itself, eons resolving into eras, eras into periods, periods into epochs, epochs into ages. The atmosphere, I discovered, became oxygenated two billion years ago. The appearance of cells with nuclei followed 200 million years later. Multicellular life made its debut one billion years ago. Another half billion years passed before fungi, algae, and most modern animal phyla arrived. Then plants appeared on the land, followed by millipedes and other creeping oddities. After this, the jawed fishes emerged (I had not known there were other kinds) along with seed-bearing plants (same response). Strange kingdoms waxed and waned. Trilobites declined and primitive trees appeared. Insects took to the air. Then, 250 million years ago, 95 percent of all life was lost in a colossal mass extinction. Out of the remnant the dinosaurs rose to dominance. Nearly 200 million years later they too vanished abruptly. With the large reptiles out of the way mammals had room to flourish and flourish we did, even to the point of a tiny unremarkable pair of us sitting on a sofa in a climate-controlled ranch-style dwelling, gazing down at the spectacle of the past in a Time-Life book.

I was stupefied. The timeline seemed a thing of great elegance. The words—*Ordovician, Silurian, Eocene*—were themselves discoveries, whatever they meant. Looking over the edge of time's precipice thrilled me. I carried the Time-Life book to bed at night and pressed the structure of the past into the soft clay of my young mind, inventing mnemonics for the periods and epochs and rehearsing them to myself until I fell asleep. It was fun.

But it was also secretly scary. The details eluded me but I got the point: I was nothing. All of this had *really happened.* The thought of life and death spread over such an unfathomable span of time— without a single human witness—was hard to accept. In the face of this, what was I? What was my life? And the lives of those I loved? Why were we here now, after all of this? It made me feel like a ghost. Sometimes as an adult I have felt the same way, usually during seasons of stress. When it happens I almost always remember the timeline.

Thus did Dad introduce me to the wonders of natural history. But his influence didn't stop with science. He also took us to church at least twice a week, and there I was handed a different book. It had no diagrams, but right up front was a story about Adam and Eve and the six days of creation. Back at home I checked the Time-Life book. And guess what? Adam and Eve and those six days were nowhere to be found in it, not on the timeline or anywhere else. Their absence was conspicuous. Were Adam and Eve the first people? If they weren't, who were? The book didn't say. Equally disconcerting was the Bible's silence regarding trilobites and stegosaurs. On which day were these created? On which day did they disappear? And why did God let them die?

What's on the Calendar?

The mystery deepened when, in my fifth-grade Sunday school class, a special visitor presented a new kind of timeline. It was on a large poster he had brought with him. Across the top it read: THE PLAN OF THE END.

It was a full-color flowchart of the future. Based on the books of Daniel and Revelation, it was divided into three main sections: the Church Age (you are here), the Tribulation (seven years), and the Kingdom Age (one thousand years). The Rapture and Second Coming demarked these segments. Featured prominently was the binding and loosing of Satan and something about judgment seats and bowls. Armageddon was in there somewhere and biblical citations were scattered throughout. The Old Testament Saints, New Testament Saints, the Unsaved of All the Ages, the Beast, and the False Prophet were all major players, as was (of course) the Lamb himself,

Jesus Christ. Arrows indicated who would go where and when. All the arrows, if faithfully traced, led to one of two terminal stations: the New Heaven and New Earth (in the upper right) or the Lake of Fire (in the lower right).

I was intrigued, but there were incongruities. Chief among them was the fact that Dad knew a lot, but he had never mentioned the Rapture or the Lake of Fire. If something so terrible was true, surely he would have briefed us. One day I found him at his desk and asked him about it.

He looked up from his work and said, "Son, that's not true."

Well, what *was* true? If the Rapture wasn't on the calendar, what was?

This time the answer came from a man named Carl Sagan. It turned out we had a copy of his new book *Cosmos* up on the shelf with the Time-Life series. On pages 228 and 229 I found, in the form of four images and a caption, what I was looking for.

The first image shows a bright seaside: the blue sky dotted with white clouds; the ocean; an abundance of green growing things along the coast; the yellow sun low on the horizon, its light amplified by reflection off the sea. It is a scene of obvious natural beauty. The caption, however, is foreboding: "The last perfect day." The following frames show the same view at progressively later times, but, thanks to the slowly dying sun, everything changes: living things die, the sea evaporates, the atmosphere escapes into space, the land dries out and cracks in the heat. Above it all the sun, having exhausted its supply of hydrogen fuel, grows redder and larger. By the final frame it's a ghastly, bloated thing filling the sky above an airless wasteland. All these things will happen, wrote Mr. Sagan, "several billion years from now."

I believed it immediately.

Several billion years is a very long time but this fact did nothing to soften the existential blow. It deepened the mark left by the

Time-Life book, and I became obsessed with the distant future. On one occasion I stood inches from my house and looked closely at the bricks and wondered: On what precise calendar date will these bricks be separated? Because one day they will be, and for a fact. I looked up. What would be the exact configuration of the clouds at the moment the bricks broke apart? When would the streets of Atlanta be emptied of cars? It seemed impossible, but I knew they would be emptied eventually, and for a fact. A few years earlier I had watched the city's tallest building at the time, the Peachtree Plaza, rise. When would it fall? I pondered these questions with complete seriousness. It was all very real to me.

At the time I had a pretty simple idea of God. Like many Baptist children I got on my knees and prayed at bedtime, sometimes with my parents, sometimes alone. I talked to God and God listened; God talked to me and I listened. It was straightforward. But this new information challenged this. God became both more and less than I had thought. More because of the practically infinite amount of space and time and life out there, places and times no human could visit and creatures no human could know, and God was the God of all that too—of archeopteryx and bacteria and galaxies and planets and God only knew what else. Less because it was hard to see how, with a past so remote and a future so bleak, God could care very much about me. I pictured God like a balloon, expanding without end to contain all things. And the more the balloon expanded, the more it seemed to fade.

Hurt by *Homo habilis*

I'm pretty sure I was already on the road to rejecting Adam's and Eve's historicity the day Dad handed me the Time-Life book. I can't say when I started questioning this particular article of Southern Baptist dogma, but November 7, 1977 is as good a guess as any. That is the date on the cover of a certain issue of *Time* magazine. It is also the date when, for me, evolution got personal.

The magazine appeared in our mailbox and ended up in my hands. On the cover was a fellow named Richard Leakey kneeling beside what was to me a hideous-looking creature. It was apelike but also vaguely human in appearance. It had a giant head, broad high cheekbones, strangely long arms, and small dark beady eyes looking straight at the camera. It was a model of *Homo habilis*, a species that lived in East Africa several million years ago. Above the picture were the words, "How Man Became Man."

It didn't take long to figure out what Mr. Leakey and *Time* were telling me: This brute was my ancestor. Today the connection between *Homo habilis* and *Homo sapiens* is contested, but the scientific details hardly matter. What matters is that I was horrified by the thought of my family and friends and me being related to such a creature. It bothered me that Mr. Leakey seemed to be okay with this. He seemed like a nice man. I don't remember having any explicitly religious thoughts, but it all just seemed wrong. It made me sad. *Homo habilis* hurt my feelings.

Why? Why should *Homo habilis* bother a boy so much that he should find himself nearly forty years later confessing his feelings in a book? Why should an encounter with deep time make him so scared that he remembers it whenever he feels stress as an adult?

The cause may be a simple combination of ignorance and garden-variety trepidation. We arrive on Earth without knowing very much about the world, and we grow and learn in severely limited contexts. Cautious by nature, we stick with what works: our neighborhoods; our systems of education and government; our beliefs about ourselves and other people; our habits. I once read a story about a little boy who had been invited to eat with a neighborhood friend. It was his first meal outside of his own house. He noticed the silverware was somehow different than what he had at home. He was put out.

"These aren't real forks," he announced. "Can I go home and get mine?" A whole range of parochialisms need to be shed as we grow, and sometimes it hurts to lose them.

So maybe cosmic time and Leakey's hominid were just my early and difficult introductions to a larger world. But, for me at least, the problem had another dimension. I, like everyone, was born and raised to hold a certain set of beliefs. But the *fact* of my belief was only part of the problem. There was, in addition, the *content* of my belief: I had, several months before meeting *Homo habilis* and in the language of the moment, accepted Jesus as my personal Lord and Savior.

I was a newly baptized Christian, still wet behind the ears, and the cosmos was shaking me up already.

An Organ and a Vacuum Cleaner

The cosmos—deep time, *Homo habilis*, and all—presented a stiff challenge to my nascent worldview. At the time I didn't have the word for it, but I do now: *anthropocentric*. In my understanding humanity was the central feature of the cosmos. This word describes not only the rather conventional Protestantism of my upbringing, but Christianity as a whole. It, unlike many of the Eastern traditions, assigns us a pivotal cosmic role. You probably don't need convincing: Christianity says that human beings—and not other creatures—are made in the divine image; God protects Adam and Eve using the skins of dead animals (did God have to kill them?); God takes on human form and tells us we are more important than the lilies of the field and the birds of the air; and, as Shane Claiborne likes to say, scripture may begin with a garden but it ends with a city. In short, Christianity says that God is uniquely interested in human beings. God's love for us is the faith's central theme and the driving force behind scripture and tradition alike.

Accordingly, the nonhuman cosmos is not the central object of God's concern. It is true that God made the cosmos and called it good; it is true that all traditional creeds begin by proclaiming God as Creator; it is true that, in the person of Jesus of Nazareth, God entered the cosmos. But in all this the cosmos itself is only a backdrop to the real drama, a drama with only two players: God and humanity.

Christianity, in short, is not only anthropocentric; it is *irreducibly* so.

Perhaps this is how it should be. Perhaps the details of the cosmos don't matter in the end. It has been argued, sometimes by the most eminent of theologians, that religion and science are such different things that they really don't belong in the same room. Perhaps comparing them is like comparing, in the words of Karl Barth, an organ and a vacuum cleaner (I wonder which is which for Barth). In this view the anthropocentrism of Christianity is perfectly appropriate because Christianity is about nonhuman affairs like quantum mechanics is about salvation: not at all. Christianity, properly understood, is about *human* history and God's role in it.

There is a certain appeal to this view. After all, we are subjects, not objects, and in the end our concerns reduce to human ones. Therefore Christianity, a solution to a human problem, is rightfully human-centric. Moreover, because human nature shapes whatever it touches, including science, we should know ourselves first. It is unavoidably so and there is no evading it.

But what does it mean to know ourselves? Whatever else we are, we are creatures. Does not our history and our context *as creatures* matter? Can theology afford to insulate itself from science, which is, as the UK's Astronomer Royal Martin Rees put it, the one truly global culture? Should my theology of creation—and therefore my entire theology—be sealed off from our best scientific understanding of creation, even when that understanding threatens to upend my theology?

Is This What Love Looks Like?

A few years after my Adam-and-Eve epiphany, I took tenth-grade biology. The class started off nicely. I liked the smells of the labs, and the investigations into fetal pigs and sheep eyeballs were enthralling. There are surprising things going on inside animals, colorful, organized things. In biology as in much of nature, beauty begins at the surfaces and compounds rapidly beneath.

Except when it doesn't.

My desk was in the front on the far side of the chalkboard, near the tall south-facing windows. Directly in front of me stood a large wood and glass cabinet. It housed numerous dead creatures preserved in jars, many filled with formaldehyde. There were small animals: mice, chipmunks, snakes, crustaceans. Also some larger ones: a chinchilla, a ferret, a baby fox. The animals were fun to look at when my attention wandered from the topic at hand. Through the windows, sunlight fell on the cabinet and reflected off the liquid and glass, making the scene spectral and mesmerizing and strange.

One day I saw something new. It was a jar that contained what appeared to be a kitten, but the refracted sunlight collaborated with my angle of vision to produce a strange illusion: the animal appeared to have two faces. When the bell rang I walked up for a closer look.

There had been no illusion. The kitten was covered with fur and had two tiny faces on its head. Its four eyes and two mouths were clearly visible. The corner of the right face's left eye just touched the corner of the left face's right eye.

The teacher, Mrs. Feinburn, walked over and began talking about it. She told me it lived a couple of weeks before it died, mentioned the word *diprosopus*, and addressed the relevant genetics. I listened as nicely as possible but felt suddenly and overwhelmingly sad and tired, as if everything was for nothing. Looking back it seems strange that I was so affected. I had seen the two-headed snake at the

Georgia Capitol and also, near a family vacation spot, the grave of a newborn child. But those didn't affect me like the kitten did. They didn't make me feel as if the sum of all effort—mine and everyone else's—was zero. It was an irrational thought, perhaps, but there it was. I guess I was ready to be bothered.

Mrs. Feinburn's words only dug the hole deeper. Scientifically diprosopus is just something that happens. Weak and malformed creatures are as sure to appear as fine sturdy ones. They're just less common. The situation is like reaching into a large bag of marbles in which one out of every million marbles is blue. If you blindly select marbles long enough it would not be weird to get a blue one. What would be weird is if a blue one never showed up. The kitten was a victim of cosmic chance.

The genetic randomness that led to the kitten's trouble is firmly established in the fitful and chaotic quantum world—the world of atoms and molecules—where probability, not certainty, prevails. Such microscopic unpredictability rules our own physiology also, but the random nature of things is not limited to biology. The fabric of the cosmos itself seems to be woven with the threads of chance, and on all scales of space and time.

Sometimes the randomness is meteorological. About ten years ago a certain tree fell across an Atlanta street during a storm. It landed on a man's SUV and killed his wife and two young children outright. He was untouched. Sometimes it is seismic. The Indian Ocean tsunami of December 26, 2004 was produced by the slippage of a tectonic plate about 20 miles below sea level. It killed well over 200,000 people. Sometimes it is astronomical. At some remote time in the past a six-mile-wide asteroid was gravitationally nudged out of its orbit between Mars and Jupiter, fell into the inner Solar System, and eventually collided with Earth near what is today called the Yucatan Peninsula. This was about 66 million years ago. This impact triggered the so-called Cretaceous-Tertiary (K/T) extinction event which brought an end to the dinosaurs and allowed the mammals to multiply and grow in size. Bad news for *T. rex* and good news for us. Some lose and some win and there doesn't seem to be much sense to it. That's how chance works.

All of this seems to fly in the face of providence, the orthodox Christian idea that God is somehow in control of everything, that divine guidance and care ultimately rule the cosmos. It may be argued that "providence" is a not a scientific term and no experiment or observation could in any sense disprove it. This point is well taken. Indeed, many theologians believe that God purposefully directed (and still directs) evolution—including the K/T extinction—toward an outcome that does include precisely us. Roman Catholic theology, for example, considers evolution to be a secondary cause through which God, the primary cause, has acted to bring about the current biological state of things. Sometimes theology of this kind is conflated with the notion that evolution is inherently progressive and inevitably builds finer and finer creatures. The broad appeal of this idea can be seen in the popular line-of-primates images showing our humpbacked ancestors gradually growing and raising their heads and straightening their backs and eventually walking upright: Us, at last!

But this conceit may be an artifact of our self-centeredness and the general optimism of a scientific age. It may not correspond to any innate progressive tendency of evolution itself. Biologists are split on this question. But let's be generous. Even if we *are* meant to be here and even if God did "use" evolution to that end, God has made a strange and even troubling choice.

Evolution is an inefficient choice: only one in a thousand species that have ever existed exist today. Is this really the free decision of an omnipotent God? Why so much trial and error? It's a drawn-out choice: recorded human history is to cosmic time as three minutes is to ten years. It's a brutal choice: The K/T event is one of five major global extinction events in Earth's history, and not nearly the largest (and there have also been a number of smaller extinctions). These extinctions exhibit no pattern in frequency and no one knows what caused most of them. But we can be sure that during them the level of animal suffering, significant in the best of times, was extremely high.

This has gone on for *billions* of years. It is hard to believe that we are the reason for it.

There is such a profound disharmony between natural history as we know it and any traditional meaning of "divine care and guidance" that all efforts to bring them together seem to me to be mistaken at best and dishonest at worst. Is this really what love looks like? It seems that things could be simpler, less wasteful, and more reflective of God's great and particular affection for us. If Christianity is true, there must be *some* kind of match between its message and the cosmos God has made.

Falling Alone

The Time-Life timeline and Sagan's dying sun made me feel like a ghost. *Homo habilis* shocked and offended me. The kitten with diprosopus made me feel that all is vanity. As a boy I had no words for any of it, but without exception these encounters opened up a dark and empty and secret place inside me. They simultaneously resonated with me and frightened me in a way that only true things can. And together they called God's existence, or at least God's relevance, into question.

I had a nightmare around the time of the Adam-and-Eve epiphany. In it, I was standing in my bedroom in the basement of our house and the floor gave way under my feet. My hands clutched but came up empty. Floorboards and scraps of carpet fell with me into an abyss where earth should have been. Soon I was falling alone. I looked up and saw a tiny patch of ceiling getting dimmer and farther away and it eventually disappeared. I was still falling when I awoke. I immediately knew it was about God not being there. To this day it is the most terrifying dream I've ever had.

Even so, my admiration for the cosmos, especially for its remote and alien and threatening aspects, continued throughout high school. When I finally abandoned my faith in college I did so because the whole Christian scheme as I understood it—*God made us good but we screwed it up and so God sent Jesus, who was really God, to die for us and make us again good enough for God*—seemed small and insufficient and irrational in the face of the cosmos I had come to know and love. This view was only reinforced by my decision to study physics. And by the time I was a sophomore in college my faith, like the ballooning God of my childhood, had simply faded away.

CHAPTER 2

OBSOLETE COSMOS, OBSOLETE GOD

Thirty years ago it was unusual for a Baptist to stick out any-where in the Deep South, but at Marist School in Atlanta, from 1980 to 1986, I felt pretty exotic. Not that anyone gave me a hard time about it, but Mom had placed a fish-shaped "Jesus" bumper sticker on the 1973 Pontiac Catalina in which my brother and I commuted. This was not standard practice for my Catholic peers, so my religious pedigree was kind of hard to hide.

I attended Mass every month and, though I sat out the Eucharist, came to admire the system of it. What I loved most was the complete lack of pressure to feel anything. There were no emotional appeals and no invitations to make Jesus my personal savior today, *right now*. The liturgy was the thing, not my personal response at any given moment. This was a relief. Catholic worship seemed, contrary to popular Baptist opinion, straightforward and no-nonsense. The ritual was calming and it worked by repetition over time. It was easy on the nerves. Every now and then I still find myself coping with bouts of Catholic envy.

Though I did not do well academically, I am grateful for the religious education I received at Marist. I credit a Christian history course for priming my happy encounter with historical theology as a forty-something seminary student. There was also a class called "Biblical Archaeology," in which points of compliance and noncompliance between the biblical record and archaeology were pointed out. Mr. Huff, our teacher, loved to share grisly details of Canaanite wars and tell stories about inept Judean monarchs.

Then there was the king daddy of them all, Fr. Cavanaugh's philosophy class.

Meet the New God, Same as the Old God

It was there I met a new God, or, rather, the old one in pure conceptual form: the God of classical theism. This was not the touchy-feely Baptist God that I knew from church and home. This was the philosopher's God, the ultimate abstraction: a being omniscient, omnipotent, simple, and transcendent. Fr. Cavanaugh took us through Thomas Aquinas's five proofs of this God's existence, and we spent several class periods arguing about just why exactly this all-knowing, all-loving, self-satisfied, and all-powerful deity would bother to make the world and then let it languish, as it so obviously does, in misery and strife.

It was fun. This was new to me, a God that could be thought about and argued over and not just felt in your heart, a God I could pick up and turn over in my head and inspect from different angles. Again I felt the relief offered by the *system* of Catholicism. Its higher philosophical abstractions buffered me. They were companionable. With them I no longer had to meet God all alone.

Later in college I nearly declared a major in English. I eventually switched to physics, but I ended up taking more literature classes than most students. In one of these, we read large sections of Dante's *Divine Comedy* (including the entire *Inferno*; hell is so interesting). If you don't remember, in this greatest of all medieval poems Dante is given a tour of the cosmos of his day, from the nine-circled Inferno below to Mount Purgatory to the heavens and the Empyrean above. I remember my teacher, Bettie Sellers, drawing the whole scheme on the board. It looked like the cross-section of a great cosmic onion, with the concentric circles of hell inside the earth and the nested spheres of heaven above it. She told us how Dante's afterlife locations of notable souls and their varied punishments and states of blessedness give us a clear look into the morality of the medieval world: Attila the Hun is found in hell's seventh circle, reserved as it is for the violent, and Thomas Aquinas resides within the sphere of the Sun, which symbolizes the light of theology.

She also pointed out that Dante's cosmos was not merely religious. It was also, in its day, scientific, based largely on the work of Aristotle. And aside from its bringing together of science and theology, the complexity of this cosmic model is balanced by its overall unity. Its multiplicity of parts works together to create a whole. The medieval cosmos is an integrated view of reality, a *system* if ever there was one.

I loved it. Somehow I got my hands on a large poster of the thing and put it up on my dorm room wall. It showed souls beatified and condemned alike, angels and demons, saints and sinners, all in their appointed places, from Satan half-buried in hell's cellar floor to God the Father, a radiant point perched at the summit of the Empyrean. (Sadly, I have no idea what happened to that poster. I'd love to have it now.) But looking back I see that the medieval cosmos appealed to my love of system, just as the Mass and the God of classical theism had during my high school years.

Therefore it should not have surprised me when, upon entering seminary as a forty-year-old, I felt powerfully drawn to medieval theology. Never has there been a grander conception of God than that of the Scholastic theologians, and never has theology been so systematic and self-contained. In these ways medieval theology was like the old cosmos itself. This is no surprise—it was produced by the same age. In fact, the medieval cosmos and the God of classical theism are so well matched that I cannot think of one without thinking of the other.

"What suggests a cosmology, suggests a religion," wrote Alfred North Whitehead.[1] In other words, it's natural and good to seek some level of harmony between the Creator and the creation, to look for a reflection of the divine nature in the nonhuman world. This is exactly what our medieval forebears did, and in the end their cosmos became a natural home for the God of classical theism.

Mrs. O'Brien's God

Terrence Malick's *The Tree of Life* is an extraordinary film. It tells the story of a boy, Jack O'Brien, growing up in Waco, Texas, in the 1950s. Near the beginning of the movie there is a fifteen-minute sequence showing small scenes from Jack's early childhood. They are unrelated but crystal-clear, the way early memories come back to us. One of these passes by so quickly and quietly you could miss it: the boy, a toddler in the scene, is whirled about by his mother under a luminous early-evening sky. In the midst of the joyride she stops, props him in one arm, and points toward the sky with the other. She smiles and says, almost under her breath, "That's where God lives."

It's a familiar impulse: We, fashioned from dust, live down here; God lives up there. "The heavens," we call the sky. It's a kind of inherited reflex, an ancient idea carried over. The Greek divinities lived on a mountain, and where did Moses encounter God? Where did the disciples witness the Transfiguration? Up There.

The God of classical theism is the God of Up There. Its details might be unfamiliar to some, but its general shape is instantly and widely recognizable. This concept of God is the foundation of what most Westerners (Christian and otherwise) think about God when they *think* about God. Most believers could cite some of the divine

---

1. Alfred North Whitehead, *Religion in the Making (Reissue)* (Cambridge: Cambridge University Press, 2011), 126.

attributes—all-powerful, all-knowing, all-loving—that are drawn from this conception. These are fixed points in countless and otherwise varied understandings of God. They pass unquestioned by nearly all Christians. For most, to question these attributes is to question the very idea of God itself. So it may seem gratuitous to say too much about the God of classical theism.

Nonetheless it will be helpful to draw out a clear expression of this deity. It is not hard to find such. The God of classical theism is well described by this passage from the Dogmatic Constitution on the Catholic Faith, approved at the First Vatican Council (1870):

> The Holy Catholic Apostolic Roman Church believes and confesses that there is one true and living God, Creator and Lord of heaven and earth, Almighty, Eternal, Immense, Incomprehensible, Infinite in intelligence, in will, and in all perfection, who, as being one, sole, absolutely simple and immutable spiritual substance, is to be declared as really and essentially distinct from the world, of supreme beatitude [blessedness] in and from Himself, and ineffably exalted above all things which exist, or are conceivable, except Himself.[2]

This is indeed God Almighty. The words *omnipotent* and *all-powerful* are often used in place of *almighty*, but they mean the same thing: the God of classical theism is able to do anything that is not flatly inconsistent with the divine nature (i.e., God can't lie). The chief marker of divine omnipotence is creation from nothing (*ex nihilo*): classical theism posits that God created all things out of absolutely nothing, in violation of the Greek philosophical axiom that from nothing comes nothing (*nihil fit ex nihilo*). This belief is reflected, among other places, in the Nicene Creed's claim that God is the "maker of all things visible and invisible."

---

2. www.ccel.org/ccel/schaff/creeds2.v.ii.i.html.

Creation *ex nihilo* undergirds the idea that God is not a thing. The creator of all things visible and invisible cannot itself be a thing visible or invisible. God is therefore utterly distinct from the world, and *essentially* so. In other words, in classical theism God's distinguishing mark is radical dissimilarity from the world of things. God is other, God is apart, absolutely and qualitatively different from the cosmos and all things in it, including creatures, including human beings. My systematic theology professor put it to us by inverting the logic: the cosmos is everything that is not God.

Up to God

If God is not a thing visible or invisible, how does God stand in relation to things visible and invisible? By the lights of classical theism we can say that God is "exalted above" them.

Here we encounter again the nearly-impossible-to-avoid metaphor of height, expressed so gently by Mrs. O'Brien. Deep within the Western (and perhaps human) psyche the directions *up* and *down* denote quality as well as quantity. It pervades our speech: "She has friends in high places"; "Walter White sunk to a new low in last night's *Breaking Bad*"; "Things have been hard but spirits are rising."

It may be that we think and speak in such ways due in part to Dante's cosmos, within which the directions *up* and *down* were not only absolute but indicated actual qualities. To use a formula often found in books, the medieval cosmos was about *place* and not *space*. What this means is a little hard to wrap your head around, but it's important. We twenty-first-century people have an idea of space as a kind of background emptiness that might or might not be filled at different locations by things: this space over here contains my coffeemaker, that space over there contains air. Most space in the cosmos contains nothing at all. It's just "empty space."[3]

---

3. This is not strictly true. Even a perfect vacuum is filled with what physicists call *virtual particles*.

This idea is an invention of the seventeenth century. The architects of classical theism knew nothing of it. For them, *different places in the cosmos actually had different qualities* (and the idea of a vacuum was nonsensical). There were places that carried the intrinsic quality of being low and places that carried the intrinsic quality of being high. Gross and unrefined things tended toward the low places, and rarified and pure things tended toward the high places. For example, earth, the heaviest and coarsest of the elements (and not a planet), resided at the lowest place in the cosmos not because of "gravity" but because of an affinity between the coarse element and the low place. Down is where earth *belongs*. Its nature is to pile up in the low places, so that's what it does. And all directions away from earth are up, not relatively but absolutely.

And up, *way* up, is where God is. In fact, God is as *up* as you can get, as far from down here as possible. To get to God from down here you must travel a great distance and cross a couple of major boundaries. The first one lies at the height of the moon. There you pass out of our lowly realm where the elements mix in a perpetual stew, kittens are born with diprosopus, tsunamis roar, accidents happen, and everything green and beautiful dies, and into the constant and immortal heavens. The heavens are nonetheless physical, comprised of *quintessence*. This is a pure and transparent and unchanging fifth element, found nowhere below the moon.

Quintessence composes the spheres of the planets (including the moon and sun), which you pass through, one after the other, on your way up to the stars. The stars themselves all reside at the same tremendous height, attached as they are to the inner surface of the spherical firmament. Beyond that is something called the *Primum Mobile*, or prime mover, a sphere that somehow imparts circular motion to the stars and planets beneath it. Above the prime mover we cross our second major boundary into the Empyrean, the heaven of heavens, the divine world, full of spiritual (not physical) light. This world has its own levels and is a kind of mirror image of the physical cosmos beneath it. But really it is the other way around: the physical world is a dim inversion of the Empyrean, itself the truest and most real of the two worlds. It is at the summit of the Empyrean that God rests, enthroned and serene, above all things visible and invisible.

There is no disharmony between this cosmos and the God of classical theism.

It's often stated that the old model places humanity at the center of the cosmos, but this isn't quite right. We are not at the center but at the bottom. In this cosmos all things point away from us, upward to where God—unchanging, omniscient, omnipotent, everlasting, and utterly inconceivable—resides: at the true center, as far above the *Primum Mobile* as the earth lies beneath it. (See the figure on the next page.)

Cosmic Anthropocentrism

Meanwhile we slog it out down here. In fact, the medieval cosmos is bounded at the extremes by God up there and us down here. This bipolar structure undergirds the anthropocentric nature of classical theism.

It may seem strange to judge the old model as anthropocentric when it locates human beings at the cosmic low point. It is God and not us who resides at the center. We are, in a sense, encamped as far outside the walls of the city of God (so to speak) as possible. We are the most peripheral of creatures. We *define* the periphery.

Or, switching back to the language of top and bottom, we are distinct because we are at the bottom.[4] Like a rope fastened to a flagpole, the cosmos is fixed at two points: one low (human) and

---

4. Actually Satan resides at the true low pole: hell's floor at the center of the earth. But in the cosmic sweep of things the earth itself is but a point. We are so near the bottom as to actually be there from the broadest point of view, which is the view we are here taking.

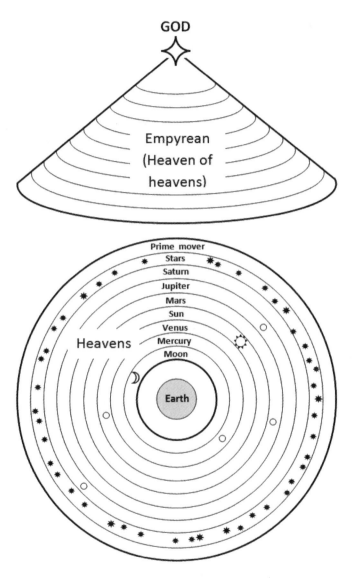

The obsolete cosmos. We're at the bottom, God's at the top. The way Dante described it, every direction away from Earth is up, and no matter which way you travel you would eventually get to God. It simply can't be faithfully communicated here (in fact, it requires four dimensions to picture it properly), but perhaps this gives you a general idea.

one high (divine). In this picture humans are simultaneously low and indispensable. The medieval cosmos and the theology that grew up with it do not work without us. Both are *about* us. Both are anthropocentric.

Two characteristics of the old cosmos further encourage this anthropocentrism. First, though it is exceedingly large, the medieval cosmos is finite. As C. S. Lewis argues in *The Discarded Image*, for most Christians in most times the statement "the cosmos is much larger than the earth" carried a simple rational meaning because the diameter of the earth could actually be compared to that of the firmament, which was for them "quite simply and finally, the largest object in existence."[5] The human world was small, perhaps, but it stood in simple proportion to the absolute. Without this sense of proportion it might have been more difficult to develop a truly anthropocentric theology.

Second, the old cosmos is static. It displays no significant or long-term changes of any kind. To be sure, beneath the moon the elements—earth, water, air, and fire—mingle freely. Fire consumes wood. Water evaporates from puddles. Tadpoles turn into frogs and frogs die. But these changes are local, small-scale, and not beneficent. Nothing comes of them in the long term. For the medieval person, life down here was more of a muddle than anything else. Additionally, there was absolutely no sense that the cosmos as a whole was changing—God had created the heavens and the earth and creatures pretty much as they were and they would remain pretty much as they were until the day of the Lord, when "the heavens will pass away with a loud noise, and the elements will be dissolved" (2 Peter 3:10).

The old cosmos was bipolar and finite and static. If it hadn't been all of these it might have been harder for the architects of classical

---

5. C. S. Lewis, *The Discarded Image* (Cambridge: Cambridge University Press, 1964), 99.

theism to maintain their focus on God and humanity. As it was, the cosmos did not distract. It remained a mere backdrop to the real show, the human-divine drama: it's just us and God.

Meet Willie B.

But that's not quite right. There are the animals to think about. Where do they fit in?

Below us, that's where. In the same way God ruled over the cosmos from on high, human beings ruled over the earthly creation. God says, in Genesis 1:26, "Let us make humankind in our image, according to our likeness; and let them have dominion over the fish of the sea, and over the birds of the air, and over the cattle, and over all the wild animals of the earth, and over every creeping thing that creeps upon the earth." Whatever it means to be made in the image of God, it at least means that we have dominion over nonhuman creatures. To be clear, however, there is no sense in which the Bible gives human beings free rein to abuse animals. Dominion is not the same as domination.

But that distinction can easily be lost. When I was a kid we used to go to Atlanta's Grant Park Zoo regularly. It was fun. I liked the Reptile House the most. It was dark and things with fangs lived in there, which was cool. But the most memorable single animal at the zoo was Willie B., an adult western lowland gorilla. He lived indoors in a cage. I guess he got bored and some bright soul gave him a TV so he could fill the hours. He watched it a lot. So we would stand outside Willie B.'s cage and watch him watch TV. We thought that was capital. (Grant Park Zoo is no more. It was rechristened Zoo Atlanta years ago and the animals were sent outside to play. Before he died in 2000, Willie B. enjoyed his new environment enough to sire five offspring.)

Such thoughtless treatment of animals is made easier (but not strictly necessary) by our belief that we are somehow superior to them, a belief given warrant by the old cosmos and the traditional interpretation of the divine image of Genesis 1:26, which goes something like this: "If the origin of the human body comes through living matter which existed previously, the spiritual soul is created directly by God."[6] These are the words of Pope John Paul II as delivered to a 1996 meeting of the Pontifical Academy of Sciences. This spiritual soul is, according to classical theism, precisely what marks us as made in the image of God. It simultaneously distinguishes us from other creatures and grants us dominion over them.

So here we sit in the old cosmos, at the low end of a staggering hierarchy. As we muddle it out down here amid the general death and decomposition, the best material image we have of God's rule over the cosmos is our rule over the animals. Just as animals cannot imagine the complexities of human life, we bottom-dwellers cannot imagine a God who rests eternally at the impossibly remote spiritual pole, opposite us in both location and essence, at the apex of all things.

Metaphysical Whiplash

Our understanding of the cosmos has moved on, but the popular conception of God has not.

We've seen the bipolar, up-down structure of the old model, but for us today there is no such orientation. Unlike our forebears, we take "up" to be a local convention with no absolute significance. There is no low place for humans and no high place for God. The medieval cosmos was of finite size and was walled-in. But our cosmos has no outer limit, no barrier like the one Jim Carrey discovered at the end of *The Truman Show*, no place where stuff ends. It may, in fact, be infinitely large. And we've seen the static nature of Dante's cosmos. Ours, however, is nothing if not dynamic on every scale of

---

6. www.newadvent.org/library/docs_jp02tc.htm.

time and space. And I've mentioned how the framework of the old model is based on human concerns. But the structure of the contemporary cosmos exhibits no regard for us whatsoever, and draws the very idea of human specialness into question. And according to the old cosmos, we are qualitatively distinct from animals and set above them, just as God is qualitatively distinct from us and set above us. But this absolute distinction and the anthropocentrism it suggests are difficult to defend within our own evolving cosmos.

In short, *humanity's vision of the cosmos has changed radically and in every way since Dante penned the* Divine Comedy.

But the God of classical theism remains the go-to divine model for Christians everywhere. It shows up not only in Catholic theology and practice but in a broad range of Protestant contexts as well. Obviously the creeds, with their leading declarations about "God the Father Almighty," reflect this God. But so do hymns and praise songs and Sunday school curricula and the everyday words of average parishioners. But this old concept of God as remote and utterly distinct, so well matched to the vision of Dante, is no longer at home in the cosmos.

Lately this thought has been occurring to me with increasing regularity. It actually produces an odd mental sensation—I call it *metaphysical whiplash.* I feel it whenever the omnipotent, omniscient, transcendent, on-high God enters my radar (which is pretty often). It mostly happens during worship. Last Sunday we sang the Apostle's Creed (yes, in a Baptist church), and I had whiplash. It also happens regularly during sermons and weddings. Religious books can prompt it, especially, it seems, when I'm studying to teach a Sunday school lesson.

It usually goes something like this: I'm sitting in worship and a fellow parishioner is speaking to the congregation about his life. The story is funny, bracing, honest. But somewhere in there comes something like, "I'm so grateful that God sent Jesus to us so we could know his love."

That does it. I'm suddenly disoriented. To some degree it's the cliché that turns me off. But underneath the church-speak is the theological formula itself—God sent Jesus—and that's the trigger. Suddenly I'm ten years old again, looking at that Time-Life timeline and the end-of-the-world images in *Cosmos*. I'm imagining the birth of the sun and solar system and the slow and indirect emergence of life on Earth. I see the cosmos in its infinitude. And I see Jesus too, walking the earth a mere instant ago when considered in cosmic time.[7] And I ask myself: From *where*, exactly, was Jesus sent?

The answer seems to be, from up where God lives. At the risk of seeming simple-minded and reductive, wherever Jesus originally came from, he is now back Up There. Scripture claims that, after his resurrection, Jesus "was carried up into heaven" (Luke 24:51) and is now, according to the creed we sang last Sunday, "seated at the right hand of the Father," from whence he "will come again." So Jesus was somewhere, then he was here, and now he's gone, but he'll be back. And apparently his travels are vertical.

I don't mean to be flip. Clearly this is not literal language. No one I know would say with any degree of seriousness that God and Jesus are up in the sky. But that's the point: this creed and others, based on scripture and deeply influential on classical theism, were framed within a cosmic model that unambiguously placed God Up There.[8] And even though there have always been theologians who have understood these words to be at least partially symbolic, until the last few hundred years they resonated with the cosmos in which they were read. This is no longer the case. Figurative language is effective only when it conforms to some degree with the general

---

7. If the 14 billion years of cosmic history were to be compressed into a single year, starting with the Big Bang and ending right now, Jesus would have walked the earth four seconds ago.

8. The biblical cosmos is not the same as the medieval, but both located God above the sky.

shape of things. It cannot do its job if it is fully disconnected from experienced reality. We need better metaphors.

The Consequences of an Antiquated Deity

The problem goes far beyond my occasional bouts of metaphysical whiplash. As I mentioned, one of the reasons I left the church when I did is because the only story I knew—*God made us good but we screwed it up and so God sent Jesus, who was really God, to die for us and make us again good enough for God*—made Christianity seem totally disconnected from everything I knew about the world. All the real action seems to occur somewhere over my head. I couldn't connect with it. It had nothing to do with me or the cosmos I was learning about as a physics student; in fact, it left the cosmos out altogether. And so I ceased to care.

I'm not alone. I regularly have conversations about church with friends and students who are not churchgoers and they tell me similar tales. Many of them are scientists or science majors, and they often acknowledge the benefits of community life offered by churches. They admire the ritual of meeting and the ritual of worship, and they see how deep friendships can form over time in the context of church. Some have even admitted to me that they are envious of such friendships. They admit that life in Christian community can provide hope and direction and even joy. But more than once I've heard that, in the end, they don't join us because they "just don't believe all that stuff."

When questioned, they admit to feeling as I once did about Christian theology: It has nothing to do with the particularity and messiness of their daily lives. It feels made-up and removed from the world they know.

The problem is widespread. A while back I stumbled upon a report from the Barna Group exploring why so many young people are leaving the church these days. The group's findings are summarized in six bullet points, including: overprotective churches, shallow theology, and hostility to doubt. Then there was this: "Churches come across as antagonistic toward science." Accompanying this are these sub-points with which a substantial number of interviewees agreed: "Churches are out of step with the scientific world we live in," "Christianity is anti-science," and "[I am] turned off by the creation-versus-evolution debate."[9]

I was stunned. Not because this is news exactly, but because science rated its very own bullet point from this rather extensive piece of research. The science-religion debate is big, sure, but big enough to register in a major survey?

Skeptical, I contacted a friend of mine who is a noted authority on these things. I asked him his opinion of the study. "Barna is uneven," he responded. "But this report seems to be the product of more thought and surveying and interviewing than most." He concluded by saying that while the bullets don't exhaust the story, they point to something real. I think this "something real" has to do with an obsolete but still-widespread theology that, before it does anything else, removes God from the cosmos.

Looking Back, Moving Forward

What are we to do with an obsolete God?

We have options. We could, as I did for a while, put God aside. Maybe it's not just the God of classical theism that is obsolete. Maybe the concept of God has become so tied to antiquated ideas that the two can't be separated. Or, more radically, maybe the concept itself is tainted at the source. Perhaps we should just let "God" go.

9. www.barna.org/barna-update/teens-nextgen/528-six-reasons-young-christians-leave
-church#.VgswhstVhBc.

We can try, but I'm pretty sure that God is the question that won't go away. Silence it here and it will pop up over there. It may show up as worship of science, or the economy, or a political cause, or ego, or an addiction, or sex, or a fellow human being—or whatever, but show up it will. Some humanists and atheists have expressed contempt for religious believers' worship of God. They ask, Why worship anything at all? One online interlocutor once asked me, "How can you put the word 'worship' on your signs? Isn't that demeaning?" I replied, "No, it is truth in advertising. We all worship something." I am convinced that not all worship is true worship, but I am equally convinced that religious believers at least acknowledge that worship is simply what all people, religious and otherwise, do. There's nothing for it but to accept it and make the best of it.

We could also try to build a new God out of the raw materials of science itself. It's hard to disagree with Ralph Waldo Emerson when he writes, "Nothing is great but the inexhaustible wealth of nature. She shows us only surfaces, but she is a million fathoms deep."[10] Isn't the cosmos astounding, and isn't the wonder it stirs in us something akin to a religious feeling? Yes and yes. Without such feelings there would be no religion at all. But are such feelings enough? Is the mind-blowing order and complexity and diversity and beauty of the cosmos sufficient to slake our religious thirst? For some it may be and I can nearly, but not quite, imagine how it could be enough for me.

Just a few minutes ago I walked out of my office onto the college quad. There in the western sky I observed a conjunction of Venus and Jupiter. At that moment, these two brightest of planets were so close together in the sky that they nearly looked like a single brilliant star. It's a wonderful and beautiful sight, and in the very best and truest senses of those words. I stood there transfixed for longer than I

10. Ralph Waldo Emerson, *Works of Ralph Waldo Emerson* (New York: George Routledge and Sons, 1883), 459.

care to admit. But in the end the cosmos, taken alone as a bare physical reality, leaves me cold. Its power and beauty is considerable, but it is not up to my personal need for God.

Therefore we seek more constraints. In our search for a new model of God we try to remain, insofar as possible, within the Christian tradition. As we shall see, it is possible to do so. There are resources within Christianity as we know it that will help us find God in this infinite, alien, and evolving cosmos our forebears could never have imagined. The Bible, in fact, has something wondrous for those who feel lost because we cannot square our old ideas of God with that cosmos. There is a story there that removes human beings from the center of the cosmos, points us toward the cosmic margins for inspiration, and encourages us to trust our own doubts and questions about life, the universe, and everything.

CHAPTER 3

THE FIFTH DENTIST

I t is 1977. Disco Danny, King of the Hustle, rules the dance floor every Saturday night. His hair is coiffed, his collar is open, and his chains are aglitter. His vest is tight, his bellbottoms are pressed, and his moves are perfect. He is the envy of everyone under the mirror ball.

He is also, as it turns out, a discerning chewer of Trident sugarless gum. Trident, he claims, helps him "watch his step." But there's more to it than that. Danny's choice of gum proves that he's got all the right moves when it comes to oral hygiene: "Four out of five dentists recommend sugarless gum for their patients who chew gum." So claimed advertisers selling Trident sugarless gum to TV audiences from the late 1960s through at least 1980. I remember this line—and Danny—from my childhood.

But it wasn't until years later that I heard someone ask the most obvious of questions: What's up with that fifth dentist? The four are easy enough to understand: of *course* they prefer sugarless gum for their patients—they're *dentists*. But what kind of actual dentist, with credentials and all, would *not* recommend sugarless gum for their patients who chew gum? Do state dental boards let their licensees get away with that? Isn't someone in control here?

This is a great mystery that must be investigated. Therefore if you were given five minutes to talk to any of these dentists, whom would you pick? The fifth one, that's who. The contrarian. That's the one you'd choose. The fifth dentist is the interesting dentist.

It was Brent Strawn, my Old Testament professor, who first presented this showstopper of a question to me. He brought up the Trident ad and its tag line during his lecture on a distinct subset of writings within the Old Testament canon: the Wisdom literature.

If you step back from the Bible and blur your eyes a little, the biblical narrative arc stands out clearly enough: we are made good (indeed, very good); we manage to mess things up and we find that we can't fix ourselves; God reaches out for us again and again and eventually calls forth the nation of Israel to represent God in the world. Out of Israel comes Jesus of Nazareth, in whom God takes the step of *becoming* one of us. This somehow reconciles us to God (there are plenty of different theories about how this happens, but the important thing is that it does). We now live out our lives while anticipating Christ's return and the full consummation of history (however that is imagined—some say it's a future event; some say it's happening even now, all the time; some think both are true). On this largest of scales it's a pretty simple story, moving from intimacy to alienation and back.

But if you look a bit closer you'll see that not all the Bible is involved in the telling of this story. Some of it is not easily located within the narrative arc. Some of it looks inward. Some of it observes. It is, if you like, commentary. Much of this literature has a rather intellectual and existential tone. In some places it is empirical and pragmatic. In others it bends in a reflective and universal direction. Overall it is concerned with living faithfully within the daily workings-out of the world and therefore values observation and reason over revelation. Though seated in a theological context, it is not religious in any conventional sense of the word. But it is in the canon, and it is called Wisdom.

Biblical Wisdom literature is not monolithic in its perspective.[1] It's written from a number of angles, but for present purposes two major positions are emphasized. Like our cadre of dentists, Wisdom literature provides a majority report and a minority report. Our true interest lies with the minority. For the sake of casting that opinion in the boldest possible relief the former will be reviewed first.

The Four Dentists: Proverbs

The majority opinion is well represented by Proverbs, a book composed largely of teachings meant to steer its reader away from folly and toward wisdom. It is pragmatic—the original audience for the book was likely young men who were soon to leave home and make their way in the world. The sage of Proverbs may fairly be viewed as a patriarch, established and secure. You can imagine him sitting down at the hearth with his male progeny to tell them how to live a successful life: fear God, exercise moderation, tell the truth, show compassion for the weak and marginalized, do not let wealth go to your head, give to the poor, stay away from strange women. Do these things and you will have your reward: security, progeny, happiness.

The message of Proverbs is in some ways complex. You cannot simply take any of its aphorisms alone. For example, one might be tempted to read 26:4, "Do not answer fools according to their folly, or you will be a fool yourself," to suggest that it is best to not engage certain people in certain arguments lest you risk being identified with them or, as the phrase goes, dropping to their level. But the following verse, "Answer fools according to their folly, or they will be wise in their own eyes," warns that your silence will only build up those who

---

1. Wisdom literature in the Old Testament is comprised of the books of Proverbs, Job, and Ecclesiastes. Several Psalms (e.g., 37) are considered by some to be part of the Wisdom literature. Apocryphal Wisdom is found in the Wisdom of Solomon and Sirach.

are ignorant. Presumably the point of such juxtapositions—there are many—is to encourage a kind of balance and thoughtfulness that will lead, in the end, to wisdom.

Despite such local and necessary ambiguities, however, the overall morality of Proverbs is not clouded by complexity or concentrated by paradox. A look beneath the surface reveals that the book's moral logic is undergirded by the single and simple equation of reward and punishment: righteousness leads to success and foolishness leads to ruin. This equation shows up explicitly in a number of places, e.g., 1:33-34: "Waywardness kills the simple, and the complacency of fools destroys them; but those who listen to [the Lord] will be secure and will live at ease." In other places the equation is pronounced and seems to justify even the excesses of so-called prosperity theology, which says that material gain is a sure sign of God's favor: "Misfortune pursues sinners, but prosperity rewards the righteous. The good leave an inheritance to their children's children, but the sinner's wealth is laid up for the righteous" (13:21-22).

I do not wish to make a caricature of Proverbs, which also contains more subtle expressions of its underlying moral mathematics. Moreover, the book occasionally confesses that human wisdom is incapable of grasping all mysteries (e.g., 16:1-2). But for the most part the book is exceedingly optimistic about the efficacy of human observation and reason when it comes to daily life. And its final message is simple: One who truly seeks wisdom will be rewarded with the good life, and in the most conventional sense of that phrase: virtue, prosperity, happiness, health, public esteem. If one plays by the rules, in other words, one may win at the game of life. The Lord is just, so how else could things be?

We call this conventional wisdom. It is a dentist who recommends sugarless gum. It is what you tell the kids. It is wisdom of the commencement-speech, God-helps-those-who-help-themselves variety, and it dominated the thinking of ancient Israel just as it dominates the thinking of twenty-first-century Americans, who love nothing more than winners that win big by digging in, working hard, and playing by the rules.

The underlying equation of Proverbs may be expressed *If A, then A*: If you do good then you'll get good. Follow God's commands, seek wisdom and righteousness truly, and God will grant you health, a large family, much land, and sizable herds of livestock. If you don't, then you'll have a fairly miserable life and not many people will like you. Either way you won't go to heaven when you die—there was no idea of a blissful afterlife at the time—but will end up down in Sheol with everyone else. But following the path of wisdom will ensure your good name and plenty of progeny up here on the surface.

The Fifth Dentist: Job

Let us now consider Job, two doors down from Proverbs.

Job is the book Proverbs might warn the children about. In it the equation is precisely inverted: *If A, then –A*: If you do good, if you are blameless in God's sight, if you are morally irreproachable, if you seek righteousness truly, then God will kill your family, destroy your house, obliterate your livestock, and kick your sorry ass up and down the stairs. Okay, maybe not God *exactly*, but God will at least stand by and watch while another, less powerful entity, kills your family, destroys your house, obliterates your livestock, and kicks your sorry ass up and down the stairs. A strange and troubling word to be sure, but that is to be expected: Job, after all, is none other than our fifth dentist.

Because we are largely concerned with Job, it will pay to take a close look at this darkest and most cantankerous book of the Christian canon.

Job Loses Everything but His Cool

We meet our hero under clear skies. The standard wisdom has played itself out just as Proverbs said it would: Job, our model of righteousness, has prospered. He is a good man, the best of men really, exemplary in every way. He makes his home in the land of Uz, far beyond the Jordan. He is an established leader, a model patriarch, the father of seven sons and three daughters, "the greatest of all the people of the east." Beyond his copious offspring he is wealthy in all the ways wealth is counted in his world: 7,000 sheep, 3,000 camels, 500 yoke of oxen, 500 donkeys, and "very many servants." He and his children live in large houses and enjoy good health. Food is plentiful and feasts are common.

In keeping with the standard wisdom, Job's material blessings are signs of his righteousness. And, truth be told, he *is* a genuinely good man, committed not only to his family and others of means but to the poor and marginalized. His generosity works with his keen sense of justice to ensure that the needs of the downtrodden are met; in 31:12-13 he describes himself—accurately—as one who "delivers the poor and the orphan" and "causes the widow's heart to sing with joy." For his benevolence and commitment to the poor he is held in high honor by the young and the aged. Nobles and princes fall silent when he speaks.

If Job is publicly judicious and compassionate, he is privately pious. He makes a habit of interceding for his children before the Lord, offering burnt sacrifices for each of them on a regular basis, so that his piety covers their sin in case they themselves fell into error. The source of Job's wisdom is, per Proverbs, his fear of the Lord. He knows before whom he stands.

Or does he? Is his wisdom and righteousness *truly* disinterested? Or are they contingent on his manifold blessings? Perhaps Job's fear of the Lord is only a byproduct of his many years living on the sunny side of reward and punishment. What, we might ask, would Job do if that venerable equation were to no longer hold? Would he still fear the Lord? Or would his prayers turn to curses? That indeed is one of the fundamental questions of the book of Job.

After Job's status as a pious and popular patriarch is established, the drama cuts to heaven. There we listen in on God's conversation with a character known as the Accuser. The Accuser—*ha-satan* in Hebrew and the forerunner of our concept of Satan—is a member in full standing of God's heavenly council. He acts as a kind of divine prosecuting attorney and is fond of walking to and fro upon the earth and searching out iniquity.

God speaks first: "Where have you come from?"

"From walking up and down on the earth," replies the Accuser.

"Have you considered my servant Job?" asks the Lord, freely, without having been provoked. "He is a blameless and upright man who fears God and turns away from evil." (Even *God* knows that Job is as guiltless and righteous a man as anyone could find.)

Try as I might I have found it impossible to read this as anything but a taunt: "You think you're good at what you do? Do you? Well, I bet you can't find fault with *this* one."

The Accuser is undaunted. He claims God has protected Job as a reward for his righteousness. "Have you not put a fence around him and his house and all that he has, on every side?" The Accuser goes on to wager that, if God were to allow Job's blessings to be taken away, the good man's piety and righteousness would evaporate. Job, says *ha-satan*, will curse God once he feels the sting of great suffering.

God takes the bet, adding a caveat regarding Job's physical well-being: "Only do not touch him." The Accuser agrees and immediately releases hell on Job's world. Marauding nomads kill his servants and steal his oxen and donkeys. The Babylonians raid his camels and murder the remainder of Job's servants. Fire falls from heaven and consumes all his sheep. A great wind blows in from the desert, collapsing Job's eldest son's house and instantly killing all ten of his children, who were happily feasting within.

Job, who knows nothing of the divine wager, is grief-stricken. He mourns his loss according to cultural convention, yet he remains philosophical. "Naked I came from my mother's womb," he responds, "naked shall I return; the Lord gave and the Lord has taken away."

The action returns to heaven, where God and the Accuser repeat the dialogue: "Where have you come from?" etc. Again the Lord freely points to Job and boasts on the poor man's patient refusal to curse God. *Ha-satan*, not to be outdone, suggests a raise of stakes: in addition to his current losses, Job's health may now be compromised. This time, suggests the Accuser, Job will surely crack. God agrees to the wager but adds, "Only spare his life."

Hideous boils appear on Job's body, covering him from head to foot. He is now poor, without progeny, and deathly sick. His wife—the one member of his immediate family who was not killed—stands by, angry and disgusted, the mouthpiece of the Accuser: "Do you still persist in your integrity?" she cries. "Curse God and die!" He refuses. Calmly maintaining that one should accept both blessings and curses from the hand of God, he repairs alone to an ash heap where he communes with his losses and scrapes his sores with pieces of broken pottery.

He does not remain alone for long. News of Job's troubles circulates and soon his friends Eliphaz, Bildad, and Zophar pay a visit. Mortified by Job's miserable estate, they mourn and sit with him on the ash heap in silence for seven days and seven nights.

One must pause at this point to formally recognize the ludicrous nature of the story thus far. God making bets at Job's expense? A divine ego battle? It's outrageous. What are we to do with it? I don't know. Several solutions have been proposed but none fully satisfy.[2]

---

2. My favorite explanation is that the thirty-nine chapters of poetry that constitute the main body of Job are, among other things, a wry comment on the naiveté of the prose prologue and epilogue, which comprise a simple folktale far older than the poetry.

So I offer none. Instead I beg you not to let this admittedly outrageous setup turn you away from the riches that await. The poetic meat of the book—up next—is more than enough to satisfy anyone who seeks theological depth in literature.

Job Loses His Cool

After seven silent days and seven silent nights, Job speaks and everything changes. The abrupt switch from prose to poetry matches a sharp discontinuity in his outlook. The scale of his losses seems to have occurred to him during the week, for his calm philosophical perspective has been replaced by existential urgency and a boiling hatred of his own life. Job refrains from cursing God and instead curses the day of his birth: "Let the day perish in which I was born, and the night that said, 'a child is conceived'; let that day be darkness!" (3:3-4). This grim inversion of Genesis 1.3 is the opening salvo of what becomes a prolonged rhetorical war between Job and his friends.

The battle is framed by the standard equation of reward and punishment. Job, like his friends, interprets calamity as divine discipline or retribution for sin, yet he's certain of his innocence and proclaims it consistently throughout thirty-six chapters of dialogue. He is therefore perplexed. Eliphaz, Bildad, Zophar, and Elihu—a fourth interlocutor who shows up later, unheralded—are not. They insist absolutely on the standard wisdom: Job is guilty of sin, therefore he had better just take the lesson and confess.

Early on, Eliphaz takes the discipline angle. He insists that God has done all this to purify Job of iniquity, that if he quietly accepts his trouble he will be blessed: "Do not despise the discipline of the Almighty. For he wounds, but he binds up; he strikes, but his hands heal" (5:17-18). Job stridently rejects this thesis, saying that if he is indeed experiencing divine discipline, it's far beyond the scale of any small sin he might have committed. And the fact is, he committed no sin at all.

His friends will have none of it. "How long will you say these things?" replies Bildad. "Does God pervert justice?" (8:2-3). Job steadily and forcefully continues to defend his innocence and eventually demands a trial before God. As Job's words grow increasingly harsh, however, the more convinced his interlocutors become of some hidden guilt. Positions harden and hostility grows as the friends attempt to protect God—or, at any rate, their idea of God—from the near-blasphemous words coming out of Job's mouth.

Three Tensions

A lot is at stake for Job. His children, his wealth, his health, and his honor have all been taken from him with no explanation whatsoever. Loss on this scale makes him search deeply for explanation, but the deeper he looks the darker things become.

Three distinct tensions are working on Job in the course of this war of rhetoric, tensions that constitute a set of foundational theological questions and threaten to pull him apart.[3] The first of these has to do with the relative weights given to tradition and experience in the deciding of theological questions; the second has to do with how to attend to society's most marginalized members; and the third has to do with the rather severe limits of even our best ideas about God.

Tradition versus Experience

Recently I was watching television with Julia, my thirteen-year-old daughter. We were witnessing a slaughter of our Atlanta Braves by

---

3. These tensions are based on those enumerated in Carol A. Newsom's treatment of Job in Carol A. Newsom and Sharon H. Ringe, eds., *Women's Bible Commentary* (Louisville: Westminster John Knox, 1998), 138–44.

the Washington Nationals. As we fell behind 9–2, the ads became the best part of the experience. One of them—I can't remember what it was advertising—was apparently inspired by the story of the twelve-year-old phenom Mo'ne Davis, the first girl to pitch a shutout in Little League World Series history, and it anticipated a future when a woman would be a starting pitcher for a Major League club. I reflexively dismissed that possibility, saying "Oh yeah, sure" under my breath. It was quiet but loud enough for Julia to hear. I knew, even as the words were tripping off the end of my tongue, that it was the perfectly wrong response. I wished to take back my words even before I finished saying them, but of course I couldn't. I apologized to Julia.

My callous remark came straight out of a tradition I did not invent. That tradition says certain people can't do certain things. It's common sense, right?

Wrong.

I didn't invent that sorry tradition, but I did inherit it. And in a small way my words kept it alive and moved it infinitesimally down the long road of history. I'm not proud of that but it's the truth.

Job's interlocutors also appeal to a tradition they did not invent in their arguments against their beleaguered friend. It's a tradition they accept without question precisely because it favors them (much as the no-women-in-the-majors tradition favors me). That tradition, of course, is wisdom à la Proverbs, the culturally approved equation of justice, rooted in the righteousness of the sages. "For inquire now of bygone generations, and consider what your ancestors have found," implores Bildad. "Will they not teach you and utter words out of their understanding?" (8:8, 10). The "what everybody knows" move appears early in Eliphaz's argument against Job's innocence: "Think now, who that was innocent ever perished? Or where were the upright cut off?" (4:7). Yet late in the argument the standard tradition is channeled through theological formulas, a sure sign that Job's friends have disconnected from what is really happening on the ash heap: "Of a truth, God will not do wickedly, and the Almighty will not pervert justice," declares Elihu (34:12).

Job, of course, is governed by the same traditional equation. In fact, like his friends he has benefited from it tremendously. To it he owes a great deal. Without his enormous stake in the standard mathematics of reward and punishment he would not be so bitter in his demands for divine justice. In fact, the intensity of his struggle is a direct measure of his investment in conventional righteousness.

But now he is forced to question the tradition that formed him, and the data that drive his questions are of a single type: experience. Job simply cannot square what he has always known to be true with his experience. It is too much—the old wineskins will not hold. Tradition says he must be guilty, but he knows from experience that he is innocent. Tradition says God must be disciplining him, but he knows this is not true. Tradition says God is just, but experience makes him doubt that God shows any partiality for the innocent (9:22). Therefore one of the central tensions of the book is between these two ways of knowing and what their relative weights should be. Job is torn.

Benevolence versus Identity or: Us versus Them

Here in Atlanta there's a long straggly fellow who's always hanging around a particular interstate exit ramp. He holds up signs asking for financial help. He doesn't walk up to my car. He just stands there, four feet away, looking at me. I usually don't give him anything. I also don't look back. I sit and stare at the light, praying for green. When the light finally changes I hit the gas and turn the corner and immediately I feel better.

I do not give because I rarely carry cash. If I did, I would give him some and I would feel better immediately. Also, I do not look at him. Why? This is trickier. I do not look at him because in my heart I believe he is a mirror, and if our eyes meet I might actually identify with him. I might see that there's far less than four feet keeping us apart. I might meet him in his poverty and humanity. That's a terrible risk to take, because if I were to do that, where would that leave me? I've worked hard to get where I am, etc.

Before his day of calamity Job gave (and felt better immediately). He provided enormous financial support for the poor, and especially for widows and orphans and others who were unattached to households. By "households" I mean families under the leadership of a powerful, land-owning elder male. Job, as the exemplar of such, was expected to give generously to the poor and that's exactly what he did. This was, in fact, the key to his righteousness and the great honor bestowed on him by all. It was not the fact of his wealth that made the nobles and princes fall silent when Job spoke; it was his tireless support of the marginalized of Uz.

Those days are now over, and Job has nothing to give. Chapter 29 is an extended lamentation in which Job pines for the golden days when he was a good and charitable citizen, when he had resources. He supplied what was needed and was loved for it—and how he loved being needed! "I was eyes to the blind, and feet to the lame. I was a father to the needy. They waited for me as for the rain, they opened their mouths as for the spring rain" (29:15-16, 23).

Job is pointedly *not* an everyman. His former position at the crown of the social pyramid is essential to the story, for he finds himself suddenly in the opposite location. The inversion is exact. He longs for bygone privilege, but is now stuck below even those he once protected. Regarding them he cries, "But now they mock me in song; they abhor me; they do not hesitate to spit at the sight of me. They have cast off restraint in my presence. The rabble rises up; they send me sprawling" (30:1).

The social system that once buoyed Job looks very different from below. It has turned on him in ways he could not have imagined from his former perch. Its pent-up angers and resentments, unperceivable from above, are loosed all round him and he cannot accept it. Instead, he rails against God for the terrible inversion of his fortune. The tension is extreme. Like me on the exit ramp, staring at the red light, he wants to *give* to the poor, not *be* one of the poor.

Maintenance versus Loss of Divine Models

Over the last fifteen years we've collected a tall bookcase full of children's books. Some of them are religiously themed. One of these in particular I do not like to read. Written by Max Lucado, it is called *Just in Case You Ever Wonder*. The theme is simple: *You are special.*

In it Lucado talks to his young daughter about things God once did. "Long, long ago God made a decision—a very important decision—one that I'm really glad He made. He made the decision to make you. . . . That's why you are so special. God made you." He also talks about things he himself once did. "Your first night with me I heard every sound you made: I heard you gurgle, I heard you sniff, I heard your little lips smack. I heard you cry when you wanted to eat, and I fed you." He talks about what he will do in the future. "I'll always love you. I'll always hug you. I'll always be on your side." He also talks about what God will do in the future: "In heaven you are so close to God that He will hug you, just like I hug you." Sentimental, of course, but appropriate for the youngest among us.

Assuming Lucado believes what he writes, however, it's clear that he has created God in his own image: a loving, attentive parent. It's not easy to see where Dad ends and God begins. God protects you and Dad protects you. God hugs you and Dad hugs you. God will always be there for you and Dad will always be there for you. God makes choices in your interest and Dad makes choices in your interest. It's in this latter mode that fissures appear in Lucado's self-styled model of God: "God wanted to put you in just the right home . . . where you would be warm when it's cold, where you'd be safe when you're afraid, where you'd have fun and learn about heaven. So, after lots of looking for just the right family, God sent you to me."

This isn't right, and all grown-ups know it. By this logic God doesn't care at all about where lots of *other* children end up, children who are born addicted to drugs, or who are abused, and so on. You just can't believe the one without also believing the other.

I still read the book for our youngest, who chooses it often enough. It's for children, not adults. You have to start somewhere. So I read it. But every time I do, I can hear Job laughing.

He laughs because he knows the folly of making God in his own image. He did exactly that for many years. But he wasn't a child, nor did he address children. He was a very grown-up and influential patriarch at the summit of the social order and acted as though God was basically like him: judicious, compassionate, sage, resourceful, devoted to serving the poor. To be fair, if he was confined to modeling God on any individual person, he chose well. It's hard to blame him for patterning God on the human being singled out by the true God as uniquely blameless and upright. It is a good model as models go. It served him well for many years.

But Job's losses expose the limits of this model, and he struggles to maintain his self-styled divine concept even as its foundations crack. He remembers his own fair judgments, rendered within his own household, and insists that God do the same with him. "Did I ever brush aside the case of my servants, man or maid, when they made a complaint against me? What then should I do when God arises; when he calls me to account, what should I answer him?" (31:13-15, JPS). Job insists that he himself has granted his servants full protection—which he has. Should not God treat Job just as fairly? He recalls his public judgments at the city gate: "I put on righteousness, and it clothed me. My justice was like a robe and a turban" (29:14). Thinking that God is, like him, a fair and rational and compassionate judge, he resorts to legal language throughout the book. At times he explicitly demands a trial before the divine bench: "I would speak to the Almighty, and I desire to argue my case with God. . . . I have indeed prepared my case; I know that I shall be vindicated" (13:3, 18). In passing his own judgments he consistently treated the outcast with care: "If I have withheld anything that the poor desired . . . If I have raised my hand against the orphan . . . then let my shoulder blade fall from my shoulder" (31:16, 21-22). Yet God is brutal: "You [God] have turned cruel to me; with the might of your hand you persecute me" (30:21). Job has nowhere to turn; he is losing his God. And it's a hard moment when your best idea of God collapses, because for that same moment it looks for all the world like it is *God* that's collapsing.

Job is at the end. He has lost his family, his wealth, and his health. The tradition of wisdom that formed him and made him good is threatened in the face of raw experience. The social system he once ruled has turned on him. His generosity toward the poor, which once brought him respect among his people, is beginning to look like mere paternalism. And finally, his very idea of God is cracking under the burden of his losses. He is on the edge of losing his mind and his God along with it. He longs for death.

Then God speaks.

CHAPTER 4

AN ASH HEAP WITH A VIEW

The Lord answers Job out of the whirlwind.

Immediately it's clear that God is not interested in the particulars of Job's grievances. Nowhere does God engage the repeated complaints, theological questions, and cries for justice that fill the preceding thirty-six chapters. This, the longest divine speech in the Bible, goes on for 125 verses and respects virtually no conventional religious or theological categories. There's no mention of worship or sin or guilt or sacrifice. Neither the law nor the prophets appear, nor does human wisdom or righteousness. God makes no comments about repentance, forgiveness, atonement, or love. Most conspicuous is God's silence regarding the ideal sought by Job: justice.

So what does God go on about for so long? The foundations of the earth. Wind and stars and rain. Also ostriches. Feral donkeys make a strong showing. Monsters of land and sea are praised.

God, that is, takes Job on a (most unexpected) tour of the cosmos.

The Tour, Part 1: Establishing the Cosmic Context (38:1-38)

Unexpected or not, as a tour of the cosmos it starts off conventionally enough: with the earth and sea and sky. An exhibition of sheer scale tells Job something he already knew: it was God, not Job, who established the cosmos, who separated night and day into darkness and light, who bounded the sea, who fixed the stars in their places. It is God, not Job, who comprehends the expanse of the earth, who commands the dawn, who sends forth the rain. The message is clear: the cosmos far exceeds Job's dominion, just as God far exceeds Job.

These themes and images recall Genesis 1. Here as in Genesis the large-scale structure of the cosmos, reflective of divine wisdom and knowledge, contextualizes human concerns in a straightforward way. These verses orient Job just as scripture itself is oriented by Genesis 1, and they represent a variation on a standard biblical theme: What are human beings that you are mindful of them? (Psalms 8:4).

But Job casts the theme darkly. This is not a chatty walk-through. It is not entertaining, inspiring, or "interesting." It is a hard ride through the cosmic outlands led by a guide who is neither obliging nor decorous. The whirlwind blows hotly in Job's face. It is time for him to toughen up. "Who is this that darkens counsel by words without knowledge? Gird up your loins like a man. I will question you and you shall declare to me" (38:2-3) are the first words out of the whirlwind. God is readying Job for battle—with God.

Thus prepared—or not—Job is transported first to the cellar of the world: "Where were you when I laid the foundations of the earth? Who determined its measurements? Who stretched the line upon it? On what were its bases sunk?" (38:4, 6). The emphasis is not only on Job's ignorance but on the stability of things—the divine architect has built the cosmos on rock. It will not be moved. Once the groundwork is established, Job is transported to the edge of the sea (38:8-18) and sent upward to the storehouses of rain and snow and hail (38:22-24, 28-30). The opening sequence climaxes in a mindbending ride through the night sky (38:31-33), which God closes with a final rhetorical question: Does Job know the ordinances of the heavens?

No, but God does, and this brings us to an important point. Earlier I said that virtually all standard theological categories are absent from the divine speech. Virtually—God *does* have a lot to say about one traditional theological idea: God. Divine transcendence, implicit in Genesis, is drawn explicitly here. God's awesomeness is trumpeted obviously and consistently and is set in clear contrast to Job's not-so-muchness. "I laid the cornerstone of the earth, I commanded the morning; you didn't. I was in the places of darkness, I was in the dwelling of light; you weren't. I know how to bind the Pleiades, I know how to lead forth the stars; you don't." That's the essence of God's opening words to Job. And the whirlwind does not go easy on the irony: "Have you comprehended the expanse of the earth? Surely you know, for the number of your days is great!" (38:18, 21). God reads like a bully, insecure and touchy. One recognizes the frankly unpleasant deity of the prologue, and wonders again if the book of Job is worth one's time.

I believe it is. Job is here being confronted with his essential ignorance. And I do mean essential. This is not ignorance that can be filled by mere information. It is not ignorance in the sense of "I don't know the composition of Saturn's rings" or "I don't know who the ancestors of *Homo sapiens* were." As a thought experiment, suppose Job had actually taken a few geography courses and did in fact know a thing or two about the expanse of the earth—this would not limit the impact of God's questions. Instead, it would only deepen the blow of divine rhetoric. To be confronted by your own ignorance can be intimidating, especially if you think you really know something. It might even, for a passing moment, make you feel a bit bullied.

At this point Job is shaken but intact. One might expect that, having cosmically contextualized Job's problems, God will now address them directly. It is time to stop talking about the elements and start talking about justice. After all, Job is a human being, made in the divine image, a member of creation's crowning race. And, small though he may be in the sight of God, he is a particularly important and worthwhile representative of that race. And justice is certainly more important than snow and hail and stars. Moreover, Job's grievances are perfectly reasonable.

"Yes," Job may say, "all these things are true. Now that I have been put in my place, can we please move on to Issue A?"

The Tour, Part 2: Where the Wild Things Are (38:39–39:30)

No. Apparently justice can wait. The Lord is nothing if not indefatigable, and there's much more for Job to learn without leaving the bio-physical plane. But where can Job go now that God has taken him everywhere?

We—and Job—passed a clue to the answer during the tour's opening leg. Deep within the meteorological stanzas came these words, easy to lose in the high-velocity blur: "Who . . . bring[s] rain on a land where no one lives, on the desert, which is empty of human life, to satisfy the waste and desolate land, and to make the ground put forth grass?" (38:25-27).[1]

Strictly speaking, this does not belong among the large-scale exhibits of our opening verses. From Job's point of view, the foundations of the earth have a lot to recommend them—if the earth were not established he would have no solid foundation underfoot. If there were no morning and evening then his life—and the lives of his neighbors—would not be ordered. If there were no limits to the sea, Uz would not be protected from the chaos of the deep. All these things are fundamental. They uphold the human world. Job and his society depend on them. They are therefore rightly praised in God's

---

1. These verses stand in contrast to Amos 4:7-8, which describe God's giving and withholding of rain in response to human behavior.

opening words. But grass in the desert makes no difference. No one lives out there, just as God said. Nothing depends on that.

Nothing of interest to Job, that is, and that is precisely the point. "The wilderness had been created as supremely valuable in the eyes of God precisely because it had no value to men . . . it offered them nothing," wrote Thomas Merton.[2] Therefore we find God's attention, and God's *affection*, directed toward what appears to be a thoroughly useless feature of the cosmos: grass in the desert wilderness. God apparently notices and loves things that mean nothing to us. God loves the remote and forgettable and inhuman with a perfectly disinterested love. But the wilderness holds more than grass. It also holds creatures, creatures for whom grass might be quite important. These verses thus foreshadow the tour's new direction: outward, toward the wild things.

As Job enters the wilderness, the tour slows. God pauses at smaller exhibits and takes more time with each one. Like a jet over a jungle, the high-velocity introduction missed details. Now individual animals come into focus. The exhibits are puzzling and, one can imagine, exasperating for Job. Instead of rising to his concerns about justice, God drops down the metaphysical scale toward creatures sometimes brutal, sometimes embarrassing, sometimes foolish, always peripheral.

God starts with lions and ravens, and the theme here is food. The Lord, true to form, is interested in Job's ignorance and lack of ability to understand or sustain these creatures: "Can you hunt prey for the lion? Who provides for the raven's young ones?" (38:39, 41). The point is, of course, that God can and does; but again, the poetry suggests more than simple power. God *admires* these beasts, not as trophies or food for human beings, but as creatures set apart, members of their own communities living at the edge of human awareness. Human beings must plant their crops and plan their hunts.

---

2. Thomas Merton, *Thoughts in Solitude* (New York: Farrar, Straus & Giroux, 1999), 4–5.

They must forecast storms and read the seasons. But in the wilderness, for the lion and raven, there is only God.

Next Job gets an eyeful of mountain goats and deer. The mountain goats, dwelling among distant peaks, give birth and God is there, a witness also to the calving of deer (39:1). As seasons pass, God observes the young animals grow strong and leave their homes and parents behind (39:4). These are intimate moments in wild lives. The Lord notices and is present to them all. Job is not—the clear subtext is that he has never once even considered the lives of these marginal creatures, so precious in God's sight.

With only one exception, the animals mentioned in this leg of the tour do not dwell with human beings. They are free creatures making their homes far beyond the human world. Considering them, Job may sense God pushing him up against the limits of his knowledge and influence. The wild ass (39:5-8), dependent on desert grass, is a denizen of the steppes and salt flats and disdains the city and the marketplace; they mean nothing to it. It loves its freedom and mocks the civilization that has been so good to Job. The wild ox (39:9-12) will not work for Job—it values its freedom too much to be dependable or faithful to any human master. These verses hint at a slowly developing cosmic inversion: from a divine point of view it might be Job, and not these animals, who occupies the outskirts of creation.

The darkly comical ostrich is awarded six full verses of divine admiration (39:13-18), more than any animal up to this point. Yet it is the most foolish creature of them all, an animal wholly free of wisdom or understanding. It struggles to fly yet is not equipped for the task. It carelessly leaves its eggs on the ground to be trampled by other animals, and when a few young do manage to emerge, the adult bird either ignores them or treats them viciously, as if they were of another species altogether. It expends itself in vain—how proud it would be if it did not! But God is happy with the bird. Foolishness too is part of the cosmos, a lovable part even. The ostrich may seem a mistake but it is not. It, with all its apparent imperfections, belongs.

Other animals follow. The war horse, domesticated but only barely, is praised for its courage and lack of hesitancy in battle (39:19-25). The hawk angles southward far above the desert plain, another turn of an ancient migration cycle Job has never considered (39:26). At the periphery of knowledge, in the remotest crags of mountain and rock, the vulture makes its home. Even grass means nothing to this sharp-eyed scavenger who lives on death and fills its young with the blood of its prey (39:27-30).

Where do these exotic exhibits leave Job? Hushed and acquainted with his limits. For the first time since the appearance of the whirlwind, he speaks: "See, I am of small account; what shall I answer you? I lay my hand on my mouth. I have spoken once, and I will not answer; twice, but will proceed no further" (40:4-5). There was a time, not long before, when Job occupied the summit of what he considered earth's central society. If the first leg of the tour scaled down human society in relation to God and the cosmos, the zoological leg displaces it from the center. Here God's attention and affection are not weighted toward the human but tilt decidedly away from it. The fringe has become the hub, the center is now peripheral. What is marginal to Job is not marginal to God. Job's anthropocentrism was sufficient while the going was easy, but it is now fading in the light of a brilliant and brutal cosmos.

The Tour, Part 3: Into the Cosmo-Mythological Unknown (40:15–41:34)

Here there be dragons.

These words, sometimes found at the edges of old maps, signaled the limits of known territory. Knowledge gives out in the trackless land marked by them. Boundary creatures are typically large and toothy and are always beyond human control (one never sees, "Here there be puppies"). And now, having allowed Job a few seconds to pause and say a quick word, God transports him beyond the boundaries for a close look at two such creatures.

Behemoth, a monster of the land, comes first. Job 40:15-24 is the only passage in the Bible that mentions this animal, leaving plenty of space for resourceful interpreters to play. Young-Earth Creationists, who read Job as historical, see in Behemoth a large sauropod dinosaur, perhaps a brontosaurus or diplodocus. Some commentators identify it as a hippopotamus, pointing to resonances within ancient Egyptian religion. But this is problematic—whatever else may be true of hippopotamuses, their tails do not in any way evoke cedar trees (40:17). Today Behemoth is often read as a semi-mythic symbol of chaos, and this is how I take it.

Chaotic it may be, but Behemoth is also awesome. "Its bones are tubes of bronze, its limbs like bars of iron," God proudly says of this creature (40:18). There is no dream of taming it, no thought of hunting it. Even God must carry a sword to approach it (40:19).

But God has no reason to do so. This passage, like others from the divine speeches, may be fairly read as God showing Job yet again just how powerful God is and just how weak Job is. But, again, this is not just a display of brute power. The Creator is pleased with the creature and the world in which it lives. Of it the Lord says, "The mountains yield food for it where all the wild animals play. Under the lotus leaves it lies, in the covert of the reeds and in the marsh" (40:20-21). This is a scene of natural balance, a vision of chaos quite at home in the world. God carries no ill will toward the monster.

Behemoth is a primeval beast, "the first of the great acts of God," and, interestingly, it is described as made by God "just as was Job" (40:15). From the divine point of view, both Job and Behemoth are creatures, cousins perhaps, occupying the same world and equally deserving of attention. That Behemoth is unsafe while Job is not does not evoke concern on God's part.

As the tour stretches out, the mythological takes over completely.[3] The pace continues to slacken and the time spent on each exhibit continues to increase. Behemoth, the strangest and most mythological creature seen so far, has taken ten verses, more than any merely biological specimen. There's also a trend toward instability: the chaotic and unpredictable quality of the monster stands in contrast to the fastness of God's initial subjects: the foundations of the earth, the fixed stars.

And, as the end of the voyage approaches, the mismatch between God's exhibits and Job's original complaint increases. There is some sense in pointing out the foundations of the earth and the regularity of the night sky to a seriously destabilized man, and it's a little harder to see how lions and hawks come in, except perhaps as diversions. But it seems to border on the malicious to show poor Job a monster that even God cannot approach without a weapon.

Facing Chaos

All these trends—the deceleration, the tightening focus, the increasing unpredictability, and the growing distance between the subjects and Job's original concerns—arrive at their limits in chapter 41, in which God hauls Job to the lowest reaches of the sea, the very realm of chaos, for a raw and very-up-close encounter with Leviathan, the supreme chaos monster. It is a descent, a kind of death, that will forever change Job's life.

Entering the sea itself is problematic, to say nothing of Leviathan. The sea represented chaos throughout the ancient Near East,

---

3. I don't think it matters too much if Job (or the author of Job) was aware of the mythological status of the final exhibits. The salient point is that these beasts were envisioned as located within the cosmos and were rumored to exist, yet Job had never seen them. They were great and terrible, whether or not they were actual.

and is here understood to be the state of emptiness, void, and disorder that ruled the cosmos before God brought order to it. Its most conspicuous appearance is found in the second verse of the Bible, in which the earth is described as "a formless void" while darkness "covered the face of the deep."

The standard reading of Genesis 1 holds that when the omnipotent God first created the cosmos out of nothing (*ex nihilo*), it was a featureless medium, empty of all structure and complexity. It was in a state of maximum chaos.

The Lord imposes order on this chaos by using a dome to separate the waters from the waters. The primordial chaos was divided and the earth was established in the resulting chaos-free gap (Gen. 1:6). In this cosmology the flat earth is completely surrounded by the waters of chaos: the sea bounds the land on all sides; waters lurk far below Sheol (the subterranean abode of the dead, similar to the Greek underworld); the waters above are supported by the dome of the sky (the firmament).[4] Dome or no dome, however, God's will was the only true bulwark against the return of cosmic chaos. At any moment the Lord could allow the waters to return and overwhelm the earth. Yet God chooses to hold back the chaos—to oppose its tendency to return—for the sake of earthly creatures. This is the meaning behind God's words in 38:10-11: "Who prescribed bounds for [the sea], and set bars and doors, and said, 'Thus far shall you come, and no further, and here shall your proud waves be stopped.'"

Whenever the sea shows up in the Bible, therefore, the watery threat lurking at the cosmic periphery is recalled. Some obvious examples are the flood of Noah (Genesis 6–9), the parting of the sea for the Israelites as they escape Egypt (Exodus 14:21), and Jonah's descent within the belly of the great fish (Jonah 1:17). The symbol is used throughout scripture, however, from the words of Jeremiah

---

4. This is the biblical cosmos, not the one envisioned by Dante. The medieval cosmos, like our own, is not biblical.

(e.g., Jeremiah 5:22) to the calming of the sea by Jesus (e.g., Mark 4:35-41). In all cases the sea threatens de-creation, that is, a return of the cosmos to its primordial uncreated state.

The present passage is another example. In fact, Job may contain the Bible's premier instance of the threatening sea, for in Leviathan is concentrated all the menace and leveling power of the deep, and nowhere else in scripture does Leviathan make such a showing. The beast, like the cosmos itself, is beyond Job's control. "Can you draw out Leviathan with a fishhook or press down its tongue with a cord?" asks God as the monster is introduced in 41:1, in yet another divine rhetorical question whose understood answer is no. Like Behemoth, Leviathan will not obey nor ask permission. If human beings are small to God—which seems to be at least part of the point of the book—they are of no regard whatsoever to Leviathan, which will not condescend to "make a covenant" with human beings as God has (41:4). It exists outside all systems of value and commerce (41:6) and cannot be captured, used, or domesticated. Terror entertains it (41:22) and it strikes fear in the hearts of the gods (41:25). Leviathan is, in a word, unapproachable (41:10-11).

Yet, as the tour reaches its logical endpoint, Job is made to approach it. He is drawn down to the monster and his face is held close as God executes a tight zoom on Leviathan's side (41:15-17). Minute details of the monster's construction fill Job's field of view. He sees that the beast's back is made of scales like "shields in rows" (41:15). God draws Job so close that he can see precisely what lies between the scales: nothing at all. Leviathan's armor is so perfectly fitted that not even air can pass between its plates, which "clasp one another and cannot be separated" (41:17). It is as raw and intimate a look at cosmic chaos as any human being can endure. In this moment Job's contraction of vision is complete and the tour's pace, once so rapid, falls to zero.

There remains a final dark flourish. In reference to the great and inhuman bottom-dweller, God closes the divine speech: "It surveys everything that is lofty; it is king over all that are proud" (41:34).

At these words Job's cosmos is turned upside-down. The inversion, long threatened, is complete. Once a righteous king, Job is now ruled by an amoral monster. Once powerful and in control, he is now overwhelmed by chaos. Once central, he is now peripheral. Once rich, he is now beset by a creature who laughs at wealth. He who once helped the weak and marginalized has become the weak and marginalized. Job has discovered his essential poverty. It had always been there, but it took Leviathan to reveal the truth: Job *is* the poor.

Now *that's* justice.

Whosoever Sees the Ostrich, Sees Me

Job's relentless search for justice has taken him to the floor of the cosmic abyss. It is in that alien and chaotic place—and not among his rich and well-educated human interlocutors—that he finds enlightenment. The highest of human wisdom is not sufficient to the question of his suffering. What is sufficient is the stripping away of all conceit. What is sufficient—and perhaps necessary—is *descent*. In Leviathan, at the bottom of all things, Job receives his answer.

Finally free and satisfied, he expresses sorrow and repentance to God: "I had heard of you by the hearing of the ear, but now my eye sees you; therefore I despise myself, and repent in dust and ashes" (42:5-6). Yet all Job saw with his eye was the cosmos: the earth, the sky, animals, primeval chaos. This was not a spiritualized flight through the empyrean. It was not an ascent into the clouds of Sinai (Exodus 24:9-18) or a mountaintop vision of communal blessedness (e.g., Mark 9:2-8) but a riotous and elemental cosmic plunge. When in this tour did Job ever see the Lord? When did his eye behold the divine? This question demands an answer, and this seems to be one: Whosoever truly sees stars, or ostriches, or vultures, or unvarnished chaos, truly sees God.

Job has chased the highest questions of theology until they wrapped around to meet the lowest and most elemental questions of the cosmos. Or is it the other way around? Either way, he has reached that point of balance at which all human pretensions fall away and one is left to see reality, which is, of course, all there ever was: the raw fact of the cosmos and the mystery of God.

The Fifth Dentist Confounds Us Again

By now we are used to the book of Job defying expectations: the outlandish wager between God and the Accuser, the mismatch between Job the patient (in the prologue) and Job the impatient (everywhere else), the surprising insensitivity of Job's friends, Job's acid anger, God's bullying harangue; and, finally, the cosmic tour and descent into chaos, so apparently at variance with Job's reasonable and heartfelt calls for justice. But our fifth dentist has saved the most startling turn for the denouement.

After thirty-six solid chapters of flagrantly defying the conventional moral mathematics of reward and punishment, Job is rewarded for his faithfulness (42:10-13). Once he pulls himself off the ash heap and cleans himself up, he gets his wealth back *twofold* from the Lord. He is twice as rich as he was before the Accuser had his way with him, and it is all at the Lord's pleasure! His siblings—not mentioned anywhere else—visit and comfort him and give him money and jewelry. He is granted a new family that looks a lot like his old family: seven sons and three daughters.

If it all makes you wonder, you're in good company. This incongruity, like the ego-fragile God of the prologue who made the wager with *ha-satan* in the first place, has for centuries left casual readers and scholars alike scratching their heads. No matter how you turn it, you can't see through it. After such an awakening one would expect Job to become a poor but beloved walker of the earth, a drifting dispenser of radical wisdom, a teacher of deep truth. Instead he returns to Uz and resumes his perch high atop the social pyramid, a location from which he no doubt supports the poor and metes out justice at the city gate.

So much for Job's outer circumstances—he dies rich and old and full of days.

We might yet imagine that he lived out the remainder of his years a changed man. One who has come face-to-face with death as Job has might no longer be distracted by wealth and power or even wisdom. Like a mystical experience that leaves one skeptical about the status of conventional belief, it is possible that Job's encounter with the cosmos disabuses him of all distractions.

There's textual evidence for an inner realignment. Job lost his children and never got them back. One's children are not money. They are not replaceable. Readers who are parents might meditate on this oft-missed point before considering the next: Job's three new daughters, unlike any other of Job's children old or new, are given names in the text. Moreover, Jemimah, Keziah, and Keren-happuch are granted an inheritance along with their brothers, an unheard-of practice at the time. Some will read this as a proto-feminist move on Job's part. Perhaps it is. But it is, at the very least, a sign of Job's newfound disregard for the expected and the conventional.

It's somehow disappointing that there is no further evidence of Job's awakening. It would have been nice to see him give away all his new money or at least sit for a while with the widows and orphans of Uz, perhaps on the street corner, perhaps over a meal, Jesus-style. Maybe he did just this. We don't know. This is all we have, and it doesn't seem like much. But what we do with it is the pivot on which the story of the cosmos turns.

CHAPTER 5

TWO-BY-TWO CAME THE EPIDEXIPTERYXES AND VULCANODONS

Job's suffering led him to ask hard questions about the relative values of tradition and experience, his place in relation to the marginalized, and his model of God. These questions were eventually answered—apparently to Job's satisfaction—by a wild and woolly cosmic tour. This vision vindicated his trust in his own experience, relativized his place atop the social pyramid, and revealed the weakness of his old anthropomorphic model of God.

For us the same elements are in play, but their order is reversed. We look through the telescope from the other end, so to speak. We have before us a cosmic vision that has not come all at once, as the result of great suffering, but which has been assembled over centuries of careful observation and study. That cosmos has a lot in common with Job's: it is alien, threatening, and monstrous, yet we find ourselves at home within it. It is now asking the questions, and they are Job's questions, updated and expanded: What to do with tradition in the face of personal and scientific experience? How are we to relate to those on the cosmic margins? And what kind of God creates a cosmos like ours, anyway?

We will consider these questions in light of the cosmos and in conversation with Job and an array of cultural phenomena, theological texts, and personal and historical narratives. We start with evolution and that distinctly American curiosity: creationism.

My Name Is LUCA

As a nine-year-old boy I sat and stared at that *Time* magazine cover. Richard Leakey and *Homo habilis*, posed like relatives at the ultimate family reunion, stared back. Today I see their kinship—which is also mine—as a tiny Job-style glimpse of reality, and I hear God say: Behold *Homo habilis*, who I made just as I made you.

But at the time it felt like an unfriendly joke. The notion that I came from such a brute seemed not only hurtful but ludicrous. I wondered, How can that even *happen*?

It can and does happen, I have learned since, by natural selection, the mechanism Darwin identified as the driver of evolution. Today it is still counted as the dominant (though not only) process behind life's gradual but certain changes. It's a powerful and simple idea: not all offspring of a certain animal, say, have exactly the same traits. Small variations always exist among features like size, shape, and coloring. Some variations are not expressed in the animals' physical appearance: immunity to disease, endurance, aggressiveness. (All of these variations are rooted in genetics, but Darwin didn't know that.) Certain combinations of traits give certain individuals a greater chance of survival in their given environmental niche, and it doesn't take a huge edge to make a big difference over successive generations. The sturdy and well-adapted animals are more likely to survive and reproduce and, given plenty of time and a world of environmental pressures that never stop changing, two things will happen: first, a species' overall fitness within a given niche will improve; and second, as the environment changes, so will a species' appearance and skill set. Species diverge when a single population is divided geographically and different groups find themselves in different environments with different sets of pressures pushing them down different evolutionary paths.[1]

It is not ludicrous at all. In fact, the whole thing has a certain inevitability about it. One of my six-year-old's favorite activities is bug hunting. She is especially fond of what she calls "leaf bugs." These are katydids, really, and they look *amazingly* like leaves. This is the result of natural selection—the less a katydid looks like a leaf the easier it is for birds to find and eat it. Of course if they're eaten they don't reproduce. The nice leafy ones do reproduce and make new leafy ones. After a while they all look like leaves. Other creatures have their own evolutionary pathways, but over time creatures tend to get better adapted and more likely to survive. It applies to humans as well—within a given environment we tend to get stronger and healthier over time. Richard Dawkins sums it up beautifully when he writes, "No doubt some of your cousins and great-uncles died in childhood, but not a single one of your ancestors did. Ancestors just don't die young!"[2]

That we have evolved from earlier species is not really debatable. Quite apart from the overall inevitability of the notion and mountains of genetic evidence, signs of our evolutionary past show up all over our bodies: our wisdom teeth, our tailbones, and certain muscles of the ear are remnants of earlier days when we had larger jaws, tails, and independently moving ears. Goosebumps are a holdover from a time—not so very long ago—when more of our bodies were covered with hair and it was in our interest for it to stand on end when we were threatened or cold. But my favorite obsolete structure is the *plica semilunaris*, the thin fold of skin at the inner corner of

---

1. If we were to colonize Mars while some of us stayed back on Earth, and if the two groups remained genetically separate, the Martians would eventually become a distinct species.

2. Richard Dawkins, *The Selfish Gene* (Oxford: Oxford University Press, 1976), 40.

the eye. This is the vestige of a *nictitating membrane*, or third eyelid, such as may be seen on many birds, reptiles, and some mammals. It's weird to think that we used to blink sideways, but we did. The history of life is strange.

And what that history has bequeathed us is incredible by any standard. Genesis tells us that God set Adam the task of naming the animals. It's one of the few divinely assigned jobs we've not totally fumbled (another: be fruitful and multiply). To the contrary, we've demonstrated extraordinary follow-through; today we have named about one million species of animals (about 40 percent of these are beetle species [!]). What's more, we've exceeded expectations by affixing names to lots of other living things too. Among these are about 250,000 species of plants and 70,000 species of fungi. Also we have named a lot of simple unicellular creatures—bacteria and things called *archaea*. We know of about 10,000 species of these organisms but they are hard to classify. The total number of different kinds of bacteria and archaea is not known. It cannot even be estimated. And none of this counts the *protists*, another large and hard-to-organize group of microorganisms. All told, by the most modest projections there are at least several million more species—animals, plants, and otherwise—yet to name. It's a big project.

But this diversity is just a snapshot. Past species must also be considered. As I have indicated, species are impermanent and fluid things, not at all fixed. Cats and mushrooms, say, do not have immutable cores that make them cats and mushrooms. Scientifically speaking, "essence of cat" does not exist. Nor is "mushroomness" a thing. Yet species do persist for a while. For animals, the average is somewhere around several million years. Some disappear more rapidly than that, and some species with us today—the tuatara (a reptile) and the coelacanth (a fish) come to mind—have gone largely unchanged for 100 million years or more. So in the great drama of life on Earth most species have long since bowed out. In fact, it's estimated that the number of species alive today represents only about one thousandth of the total across time. So a conservative count of the number of species the planet has supported since life began gives about five billion. It is almost certainly *much* higher than this.

Whence this range of life? The answer is LUCA. A pillar of evolution is the concept of the *l*ast *u*niversal *c*ommon *a*ncestor. This is the most recent organism from which all current forms of life have descended (it's hardly recent, however; our best estimates place it between 3.5 and 3.8 billion years ago). It is, quite simply, the ancestor of us all: giraffes, whales, slime molds, lichens, human beings, *E. coli*, rotifers, mosses, cypress trees, vampire squid, herons, Gila monsters. It's also the ancestor of all past species we have identified. And, as mentioned above, these different species did not appear separately in a one-by-one sense but branched out gradually over time from earlier species, and these from earlier species and, ultimately, from LUCA. In Darwin's famous words, "From so simple a beginning endless forms most beautiful and most wonderful have been, and are being, evolved."[3]

Darwin's admirable prose aside, in November 1977 the form called *Homo habilis* was not most beautiful and most wonderful to me. But I was not alone in being offended by evolution. It bothered other people too, and still does.

Cats and Dollodons, Living Together

"God sent two of every land animal into the Ark—there were no exceptions. Therefore, dinosaurs must have been on the Ark."[4] So writes Ken Ham, the world's best-known creationist. He is the President and CEO of Answers in Genesis and the driving force behind

---

3. Charles Darwin, *The Origin of Species* (London: John Murray, 1859), 490.
4. www.answersingenesis.org/dinosaurs/dinosaurs-and-the-bible/.

Kentucky's Creation Museum, whose mission is "to point today's culture back to the authority of Scripture and proclaim the gospel message."[5] The museum boasts many entertaining features: a planetarium, zip lines, a petting zoo, a café ("Noah's Coffee"). But these are so many electrons buzzing around a stable and serious nucleus, an exhibit called "The 7 C's of History." It starts, naturally enough, with Creation. Here Adam and Eve are seen lounging in the bright luxury of Eden, surrounded by animals, including, yes, dinosaurs.

Since dinosaurs were contemporaries of Adam and Eve they must have been on the Ark as well. Therefore, when Ham and company cut the ribbon on Ark Encounter, their 150-million-dollar "family oriented and historically authentic attraction" centered on a full-scale replica of Noah's Ark, animatronic dinosaurs will be on the big boat. Construction on the Ark has started in rural Kentucky, a short drive away from the Creation Museum.

There has been considerable opposition to the project, and from many directions: Chamber of Commerce types who are concerned for Kentucky's public image and its ability to attract businesses; Kentucky taxpayers who have questioned the Commonwealth's support of the park's overt religious agenda; Christians who believe their faith is being misrepresented; and a broad range of scientists, science teachers, and science advocates. They have all fought Ark Encounter in their own ways. Despite this, the Great Recession, and Kentucky's reneging on a certain set of tax incentives, the project continues to move forward.

Ham gives God credit for the continuing financial security of the Ark Park. In his view, divine providence has worked through a revived economy, an offering of millions of dollars of municipal bonds, and the Russell Crowe movie, *Noah*.

Also Bill Nye the Science Guy.

---

5. www.creationmuseum.org/members/mission/.

In February 2014 Nye and Ham publicly debated the question, "Is creation a viable model of origins in today's modern scientific era?" It was streamed live to over 7 million people and has been viewed online by many millions more. It is of course not possible to say who won the debate—that depends on whom you ask—but everyone knows who came out in better shape than he went in: Ham. "[My] debate with Bill Nye . . . helped bring Ark Encounter to the world's attention [and] prompted some people who had registered for the bonds to make sure they followed through with submitting the necessary and sometimes complicated paperwork," said Ham in a 2014 statement.[6] Ark Encounter is scheduled to open in 2016 and is expected to welcome over a million guests during its first year of operation.

The debate was sober and well managed, a thoroughly civil affair. Why did it spark such an increase in giving? For one thing, Ham is an outstanding orator and a seasoned debater. He was meticulously prepared. Additionally, many Americans resonate with his culture-in-crisis, back-to-the-Bible message. Some years ago evolution was taken out of the laboratory and field station and plopped down in the middle of a cultural and political battle. Many Christians are still sure that "belief in evolution" and a number of societal ills—domestic violence, drug abuse, pornography, and, for them, same-sex marriage—go hand-in-hand. For them, such belief is a marker for a broad range of liberal and/or atheistic positions. The converse is also true: rejection of evolution is used by some as a tracer for extreme cultural and religious conservatism. To the latter yours truly pleads guilty. Whenever I want to know where a religious college stands on doctrinal issues, I skip the official mission statement and scan the biology curriculum instead.

---

6. www.answersingenesis.org/ministry-news/ark-encounter/bond-offering-succeeds -for-full-size-ark/.

So the political and cultural appeal of Ham's message is, for a certain subset of Christians, undeniable. But I suspect that Ark Encounter's finances would not have bounced as high as they did if Nye had not been part of it, and not because he rallied Ham's base by being dismissive of faith. To the contrary and much to my point, Nye was a perfectly civil, bow-tied gentleman throughout the evening. He just showed up and did what he does so well: speak plainly and directly about evolution.

For two and a half hours millions of culturally conservative Christians sat and considered the cosmos in all its difficulty and strangeness. They were told that we are very recent arrivals on the scene and that our appearance seems to have been contingent on a long and unlikely series of events. They were told that countless oddball creatures came and went long before we showed up. They were told that *Homo sapiens* is intimately related to all other species. That is, they were given a sustained look at the cosmos through a decidedly non-anthropocentric lens. Kind of like Job.

Unlike Job, however, they didn't seem to care for such a view. Instead, they promptly recommitted to creationism by supporting the construction of a full-scale, dinosaur-carrying replica of Noah's Ark.

Dividing the World in Order to Conquer It

Ham is representative of Young-Earth Creationism (YEC), a species of creationism both extreme and well funded. YEC holds that the cosmos (and everything in it) was formed over six twenty-four-hour periods approximately 6,000 years ago. This number is determined by using the biblical account alone—with its historical markers and begats—to calculate the year of creation. Different methods yield different precise values for Year One, but all round to 4000 BC.

YEC is not a fringe group, at least not in the United States. A 2013 poll by the Pew Research Center found that one in three adult

Americans believe that "humans and other living things have existed in their present form since the beginning of time."[7] A YouGov survey taken later that year asked a similar question and received a similar result: 37 percent agreed that "God created human beings in their present form within the last ten thousand years."[8]

Although its scientific and theological positions are not defensible, it is not my purpose to argue against YEC. That has been done by many gifted writers, Christian and otherwise. Instead I single out YEC because it illustrates, obviously and on a public scale, the point I made in personal terms in Chapter 1 and in theological terms in Chapter 2: the evolving cosmos is at odds with many people's understandings of the Bible and Christian tradition. Additionally, YEC shows how at least one Christian subgroup has responded to the questions Job faced, questions that are forced on us by science. Finally, the clarity and extreme nature of the YEC response makes for a useful comparison with other views, considered in later chapters.

Experience versus Tradition: Keeping the World Safe for Creationism

> First we guess. Don't laugh, that's really true. Then we compute the consequence and compare the results to nature, to experiment or experience. . . . If it disagrees with experiment, it's wrong. In that simple statement is the key to science. It doesn't make any difference how beautiful your guess is or how smart you are or who made the guess or what his name is. If it disagrees with experiment, it's wrong. That's all there is to it.[9]

---

7. www.pewforum.org/2013/12/30/publics-views-on-human-evolution.
8. www.today.yougov.com/news/2013/07/22/belief-in-evolution-up-since-2004/ (accessed 11/29/2015).
9. www.youtube.com/watch?v=-2NnquxdWFk&t=16m46s (accessed 8/7/15).

So said Richard Feynman, one of the great physicists of the twentieth century, about science. The thing to notice here is Feynman's association of science with *experience*. It is apt, I believe. Scientists are typically Doubting-Thomas sorts of people and insist on grounding their convictions in certain kinds of experienced reality.

Another great physicist, Albert Einstein, might agree. He once said that "[t]he whole of science is nothing more than a refinement of everyday thinking."[10] If we can take this and make the not-so-bold move to say that everyday thinking is based in everyday experience, we will be drawn back around to Feynman: science is ultimately grounded in experience. To be sure, scientific experiments and observations are a peculiarly systematized kind of experience—that's the refinement part—but it is experience nonetheless.

It's clear that our pair of physicists is on to something, so we can fairly ask: How do Young Earth Creationists balance scientific experience on one hand and their received tradition of a literal six-day creation on the other? It would be tempting, given their rejection of so much science, to say that they don't bother to balance them at all.

Yet this is not quite right. They do not insist that *all* experiments and observations are wrong. They keep what they can, and are careful about the choices they make. For example, they do not argue with this amusing fact: the Moon's orbit around the Earth is a gradual outward spiral. Today the Moon's distance from the Earth is increasing roughly as fast as your fingernails grow: about 1.5 inches per year. This they accept. But reconciling this tiny slice of experience with their tradition results in strained and oversimplified arguments.

To wit: This rate of 1.5 inches per year is not constant. It depends on several factors. If you are thorough and take them all into account you find that, at the time of its creation 4.5 billion years ago, the Moon was at about 140,000 miles away (60 percent of

---

10. Albert Einstein, *Out of My Later Years* (New York: Citadel, 1956), 59.

its present distance). But if one particular factor, the motion of the continents—which also move, on average and by coincidence, about as fast as your fingernails grow—is ignored, one is led to conclude that the Moon was actually *in contact* with the Earth about a billion years ago. This date is long after the earliest forms of life appeared on the planet. It rules out evolution as we know it but allows for a recent creation (the Moon has spiraled outward less than half a mile in the last 6,000 years). Therefore the drifting-continent factor is ignored by all Young Earthers and the world is kept safe for creationism.

The tension between experience and tradition is resolved by YECers by dividing the world: some pieces of experience simply must be ignored for tradition to be upheld. All the offending pieces add up to a very large portion of scientific knowledge, and it's not a portion you can remove without destroying the integrity of the whole. Despite its scientific-sounding arguments, therefore, YEC pretty much casts out all meaningful scientific experience. Tradition, such as it is, is maintained.

Us and Them: The Wages of Sin Is Plate Tectonics

How about other troubling aspects of the cosmos? Getting evolution proper out of the way removes the problem of hundreds of millions of years of animal suffering, but there's plenty of redness in tooth and claw to go around today, just as there was in Job's time. What of the ostrich's cruelty (Job 39:16)? What of the young vultures sucking down blood, whose parents survive off the slain (39:30)? How do Young Earthers reconcile the brutality of the cosmos with a loving, life-giving God?

By blaming it—*all* of it—on us.

Answers in Genesis publishes a series of children's books called *The Answers Book for Kids*. These books answer questions kids presumably ask all the time, like "What is Satan's dominion?," "What happened to Megalodon?," and "Did we use dinosaurs for transportation?" As arresting as these questions are, it is "Did bumblebees have stingers before Adam and Eve sinned?," submitted by Heidi, age ten, that is relevant for us. Ham's answer:

> Because of Adam's sin in the Garden, we do not live in a perfect world. We really can't imagine what a perfect world would be like. We know there was no violence and no death—we wouldn't expect this from a loving, life-giving God. Our Scripture verse (Rom 8:22) tells us that the whole creation is affected by sin, and that includes bumblebees. So, when we consider their stingers, all of us wonder the same thing that you've asked, Heidi. I think it is likely that the bumblebees had what we now call stingers before sin, but they weren't used to harm anything. I am sure they weren't originally meant to sting, but because of sin in the world, things have changed! When a bumblebee reacts to us in a fallen world, it hurts![11]

I'm not a child, but I used to be one. And I'm trying to imagine being ten-years-old and having someone I trust tell me that bees sting people and other animals because Adam and Eve were naughty. And I'm trying to imagine *not* believing that if only I were good enough—if I would just stop stealing cookies and being mad at my brother and having those feelings when I look at my teacher—then bees might not sting us. And maybe animals wouldn't kill and eat other animals. And maybe everything would be perfect, which is the way God wants everything—including me—to be.

What a strange and heavy burden. And it's not just carried by children.

Job, when brought face-to-face with the brutal and difficult cosmos, heard and received the message: Not all things are about

---

11. Cindy Malott and Ken Ham *The Answers Book for Kids Volume 1* (Green Forest, AR: Master Books, 2008), 35.

you and your supposed central role in the world. There are things you do not understand; there are needs you have never considered; there is suffering even you do not know. Having accepted this divine communiqué, delivered as it was with total clarity, Job straightaway repented in dust and ashes (42:6).

But here is a group of Christians who, when faced with the same suffering cosmos, double down on their anthropocentrism to the point of pathology. This is extreme, even obsessive, human-centeredness: not only are we responsible for moral evil, we are responsible for natural evil too, even death, *all of it*. Everything that causes suffering in the world, whether directly or indirectly—animal violence obvious and inconspicuous, plate tectonics (think tsunamis), all disease, tornados—is, in the end, about us and our wickedness. There really is no Them—cosmos, animals, plants—at all, not really. There is, in the end, only Us.

Models of God: A Rigid and Sentimental Perfectionist

Which brings us to the YECers' model of God.

Just like the God of classical theism, YEC's God is infinite, omnipotent, omniscient, self-existent, etc. But this doesn't stop Ham from talking as if God is basically like us. For example, when it comes to creation, he speaks of God designing and building the human body like an architect might design and build a house. God is also compared to an artist—Ham sometimes speaks of human beings as "God's Mona Lisas" and "God's Davids," referring to the famous works of art. This kind of talk is in line with virtually all standard theology and is not particular to creationism. But it's worth noting that in this view God stands outside of creation, just as an architect and an artist stand outside their works. Their nature may be reflected in them but they are not internally related to them.

Despite its orthodox credentials, however, the creationists' deity is simple and transparent and totally above-board and therefore quite different from Job's confounding whirlwind. The creationist God avoids paradox and ambiguity and lays everything out flat and square: "If one accepts there is a God who created us, then that God also owns us . . . and thus has a right to set the rules by which we must live," reads a line from Answers in Genesis.[12] This God makes all things bare and democratic, right there in the Bible, plain as day for everyone to see, like the results of a scientific experiment. It is inevitable that evolution—earthy, inefficient, and patently unwholesome—would be inadmissible to one who sees God as fundamentally forthright and plain-dealing.

Where Job's tradition was challenged and defeated by the divine vortex, Ham's is consistently and insistently upheld by his God. In fact, the YEC position seems to write God into an odd hybrid role, one part Accuser and one part Job's friends, from which the Divine espouses conventional wisdom: "Damn your experience," this God might say. "If you critique the six-day creation tradition, you're messing with the truth. Any deviation from that tradition—which is laid out plainly for all to see, just as everyone has known forever—will land you in the outer darkness." Living under such a micromanaging God must be pretty stressful.

As I read about Heidi and the bees, I began to wonder if Ham's God is maybe a little angry. What other kind of God would crack the Earth and send tsunamis because of human mistakes? So I did some research and found an Answers in Genesis webpage devoted to answering questions about God, and under the first question, after a short statement about how God is revealed clearly in the wonders of creation, comes the organization's first definitive statement about God: "God is angry with us." Why? Because

---

12. answersingenesis.org/is-god-real/is-there-really-god/.

we are "suppressing the truth" of literal six-day creation. This is not smack talk or the surge of the whirlwind; it is "swollen indignation," full-bore divine rage directed at everyone who disagrees with the YEC view.

On the other side of this I can't help but sense a strange sentimentality in Ham's "loving, life-giving" God. This God's no-snakes-in-the-grass ethos has an uninteresting wholesomeness that seems to apply universally. It may be seen, among other places, in Ham's use of the term "perfect world" in his answer to Heidi. Where did Ham get his idea that the creation, pre-fall, was *perfect*? The text never tells us that creation was perfect, just that it was *good* and then *very good*. I'm not convinced that *very good* precludes bee stings. Ham's deity is a bit overdelicate. A fuzzy kind of sentimentality, a longing for a time when All Was Right, suffuses the YEC outlook and renders its God sweet and boring.

I have a dear friend who is a creationist, and she is evidence enough that taking a six-day stance on creation does not lead inexorably to such weird patho-theology. Nonetheless I suspect there is a deep logical relation between YEC's categorical rejection of the cosmos on one hand and the rigid and sentimental Young Earth God on the other.

Perhaps Ham and company just follow Young Earth logic further than others care to.

A Lifting of the Burden

Ham and company are not the only ones who have felt the exacting eye of God upon them.

"What are human beings, that you make so much of them, that you set your mind on them, visit them every morning, test them every moment? Will you not look away from me, let me alone until I swallow my spittle, you watcher of humanity?" (Job 7:17-20). Thus does Job riff ironically on Psalm 8:4, lamenting the burden of having God's incessant attention. The Lord dogs Job's every thought and move, and Job is tired of it.

It seems to me that anyone who believed God was reading her thoughts, waiting for her to fall outside the boundaries of strict six-day creationism (or any equally narrow doctrine), would get tired also. She might follow Job's example and give God a piece of her mind. But she might not—the Watcher of Humanity has set the rules, and they are plain. It is for her only to obey and be watched. Where else would God look? In this extreme anthropocentric view, the eye of God has nowhere else to be but right down on us, for the remainder of the cosmos is marginal.

You don't need to be a Young Earth creationist to feel the divine eye turn critical. I suspect many of us periodically feels shame about something we've done, or fears that we are right at that moment screwing things up, or regrets about some decision we've made, and senses—*knows*, really—that God is looking and *is not pleased*, that we no longer have a place at the great and general feast.

It might be a simple falling-short that does it. I once submitted an essay to a well-known publication. The response came in August, a hard month in Georgia. Everything had been baked brown and the heat was dull and heavy, no longer bracing and tonic the way it had been in June. I knew what the letter said but I stood there by the mailbox and opened it anyway. "Thank you for your submission. We are sorry. . . ." The sun burned down on me from the center of the heat-whitened sky. For a single second it became a great eye, full of attention and fair of judgment: You have failed.

That was a lie, and it did not come from God. It came from me. God is not watching us, waiting for us to fail or to sin or to check off the right belief boxes, whether those boxes say "six-day creation" or whatever. To think otherwise is to carry a terrible burden.

The good news of Job is that that burden may be put down.

In 2012 my wife took a business trip to Washington, D.C., and I went with her. We had spent three summers in the city together a number of years earlier, so we looked forward to visiting old haunts and discovering new ones. We love art, so we spent a lot of her free time in art museums.

But when we walked into the National Museum of Natural History I felt *happy*. Walking through the old Life in the Ancient Seas exhibit put me in an expansive philosophical mood, just as it always has. Elizabeth and I started at the trilobites and worked clear around to the Tyrannosaur. We covered 500 million years of (very) prehistoric life in about an hour.

We reentered the atrium and glimpsed a new sign, over on the other side: "Nature's Best Photography 2012." We walked in and were blown away. We had just stepped through hundreds of millions of years of natural history and now stood eyeball-to-eyeball with nature as it stands today. The photographs were breathtaking. Words can't do justice to the brilliant three-foot-by-four-foot images. I itch to describe the dalmatian pelicans, the proboscis monkey, the southern pig-tailed macaque, the camel thorn trees, to name but a few, but if I tried I would just embarrass myself.

To see such an exhibit as we did is to be overwhelmed, knowing that what you are seeing is a remotely tiny fraction of what there is to see now, today. And to then imagine these variations on life's great theme—and millions more we will never see even in our imaginations—rolling back through countless forms over hundreds of millions of years, *well*. This is Darwin's vision, and what a happy overload it is.

Such a view is challenging because we like to think—even when it hurts us—that things are pretty much about us. I don't mean us as individuals, but us collectively as human beings. We are the ones made in God's image, so aren't we pretty important? God was incarnated in a human being, not a trilobite or a macaque. Isn't that suggestive of some kind of favorable rank order?

Job suggests not. God is with us, you and me. God knows us. God takes joy in us. But God also takes joy in reviving parched landscapes human beings will never see. God takes joy in each and every one of those oddball creatures that came and went long before we showed up, the ones who lurched through primordial swamps and flitted through Triassic skies and slithered silently across floors of oceans that no longer exist.

God so often speaks to us through things that have nothing to do with us. One of the lessons of the Gospels is that, if we want to see Jesus, we should look to the margins of human society: to the hungry, the imprisoned, the naked, and the weak. Similarly, one of the lessons of the cosmos is that, if we want to glimpse God, we should look to the margins of creation: the remote, the impossibly tiny, the strange, the alien and inhuman.

At the museum I stood for a while in front of Jed Weingarten's white-headed langurs.[13] My mind relaxed, my breath became regular, and I remembered with gratitude these words of Andrew Harvey: "We are saved in the end by the things that ignore us."[14]

---

13. For the langurs and other images from the exhibit, visit www.mnh.si.edu /exhibits/natures-best-2012/photographs.html#23.
14. Andrew Harvey, *A Journey in Ladakh* (New York: Houghton Mifflin, 1983), 93.

CHAPTER 6

THE DARKNESS OF GOD

A few years ago Oxford biologist and noted atheist Richard Dawkins sat down with then-Archbishop of Canterbury Rowan Williams and had a nice chat about science, human origins, and God.[1] Williams is open to science so there was agreement between them on issues such as the importance of scientific literacy, the wondrous beauty of the cosmos, and the fact that religious people cannot afford to turn their backs on evolution and other successful scientific theories.

But an essential difference surfaced at the end. At issue was the origin of the cosmos and the possibility, put forward by some physicists, that it arose out of nothing and has evolved on its own ever since. With this idea in mind, Dawkins said to Williams, "What I can't understand is why you can't see [that this] is such a staggering, elegant, beautiful thing, why you would want to clutter it up with something so messy as a God." Williams agreed with the elegance bit but added, "I think you put your finger on one of the things that does seriously divide us . . . I'm not talking about God as an extra who you can shoehorn into that. That's just not how I see it." To which Dawkins replied emphatically, "That is *exactly* how I see it."

---

1. The discussion may be viewed at www.youtube.com/watch?v=HWN4cfh1Fac.

Plenty of Christians see it this way too. Take Albert Mohler, for example, president of the Southern Baptist Theological Seminary and a Young Earth creationist. He believes that religion and science are in a necessarily competitive relationship, writing that "evolution . . . represents one of the greatest challenges to Christian faith and faithfulness in our times."[2] On this point Mohler is wholly in agreement with Dawkins.

Their agreement may be due to their shared assumption that, whether or not God exists, God properly plays the role of an idea among ideas. For them, God is capable of being displaced by scientific investigation and necessarily jostles with science within a single conceptual space, like opposing chessmen on a finite grid. Their disagreement lies only in the fraction of that space occupied by each competitor. Mohler's science-to-God ratio is the inverse of Dawkins's, just as his theism is an inversion of Dawkins's atheism. Their contrast is evident and their game is possible because of—and not despite—their shared assumption.[3]

Both Dawkins and Mohler are excellent communicators and have spent years expressing their views with clarity and vigor. I admire them for the internal consistency of their perspectives and for their shared impatience with woolly-headedness. Their trust in the sturdiness of concepts is a refreshing contrast to the intellectual laziness prevalent in much of our public discourse.

But conceptual precision is no substitute for openness to the world. So often the cost of clarity is narrowed vision, and both Dawkins and Mohler have had to divide the world in order to conquer it. This division makes things simple for both men. I don't think it's unfair to say that, for Dawkins, science is good and religion is

2. www.albertmohler.com/2011/01/05/no-buzzing-little-fly-why-the-creation
-evolution-debate-is-so-important/.
3. There has not been, nor will there ever be, a formal Dawkins-Mohler debate.

bad. Or that, for Mohler, the Bible is right and science is wrong. The integrity of both views depends on not taking seriously those features of reality that fall outside these artificially constructed boundaries. Therefore both Dawkins and Mohler flatten and artlessly short-change the world.

In order to be open to the world, we must take even our best ideas about science and God lightly. This applies especially to ideas about God because, unlike the objects of science, God cannot be confined by any space, conceptual or otherwise. The Archbishop is right: God is in no way an extra. God is not "in addition to" anything.

This kind of talk makes some people—especially those who, like Dawkins and Mohler, seem to have little tolerance for ambiguity—crazy. Admirably labeled "theological doohickey postmodern BS" by one of my online readers, it is anathema to common-sense types both atheist and religious, because it suggests that we live in a state of ignorance about God. And nothing is more offensive to the modern mind than the idea of any kind of permanent, in-principle ignorance.

Unknowing the Baseball

Whether or not they are aware of it, when students walk into intro-ductory physics on the first day of class, they bring something with them. We physics teachers call it *physical intuition*. In most cases it's a set of unspoken, unconscious assumptions about the way things work, built up over years of living as a physical being in a physi-cal world. We've been walking and running and climbing stairs and driving cars and bowling and throwing balls and catching them our whole lives. Overall we're successful in these endeavors because we have physical intuitions that work. But just because something works doesn't mean it's true, and physical intuition often conflicts with the laws of physics.

I like to tell my students this story: On June 17, 2013, after a three-hour rain delay, the Atlanta Braves were trailing the New York Mets 1–0 in the bottom of the ninth inning. There was one out. Justin Upton had just singled when Freddie Freeman stepped up to the plate. After a few pitches from the Mets' Dillon Gee, Freeman clocked a 95-mph fastball into the right field stands, 375 feet from home plate, giving the Braves a dramatic late-night victory. It was tremendously exciting for me, but not for the Mets and particularly not for Gee, who had, until that moment, pitched more than eight innings of shutout baseball.

The ball was in contact with Freeman's bat no longer than two milliseconds. It was moving in excess of 100 mph when it lost contact with the bat and began its long high arc into the stands.

Here's the question I ask my class: Once the ball left Freeman's bat, what kept it going? What exactly is it that pushed the ball through the air along its path? It wasn't the bat, of course—Freeman dropped it long before the ball landed. So what force was responsible for the ball's motion once it was airborne?

Most students say that the air gave it impetus somehow, or gravity was responsible, or the spinning of the ball did it. But none of these are right because, once the ball lost contact with the bat, no force whatsoever pushed it along. Air friction slowed it down and gravity made it change direction, but neither of these, indeed no force in the cosmos, *kept it going*. A similar (and simpler) example is a hockey puck sailing across the ice. Once the puck loses contact with the stick, *no force at all* keeps it going. Friction with the ice might eventually bring it to rest but there is nothing pushing it forward as it goes. Counterintuitive, but true.

This foray into sports and physics is not about sports or physics. It's about misconceptions. Pre-Physics-101 people tend to think that wherever there is motion there must be a push or pull making it happen, but it's not so. This particular misconception, as simple as it is, is very hard to shake.[4] Some of my strongest students carry vestiges of it into the second semester and beyond.

The problem is, as long as these vestiges remain, a reliable conceptual foundation cannot be laid. So one of my big jobs as a teacher is *deconstruction*: the wrong ideas need to be taken apart and carted off so right ones can be built in their place. This notion of deconstruction is very important for our purposes, and we will often use variants of the word *unknowing* when referring to it, as in "One must unknow the wrong physics in order to know the right physics."[5] (For us the word does not mean unaware, as in "The lion crept up on its unknowing victims.")

Such deconstruction—unknowing—is especially challenging from a teaching point of view because, much more often than not, students' misconceptions about motion are not consciously held. They do not know that they do not know. They must be shown this. That is, in order to move forward, they must come face-to-face with their ignorance.

Unknowing, Turned Up to 11

You can unknow God also, but unknowing God can be more painful than unknowing physics.

In his best-known work, *Dark Night of the Soul*, the sixteenth-century Carmelite friar St. John of the Cross describes something

---

4. This exact misconception made it hard for our forebears to see how the Earth could orbit the Sun; they thought it needs a force pushing it along in the direction of its motion, but it does not.

5. The word "unknowing" has been used in religious contexts for centuries, and that's why we use it here. Its most conspicuous appearance is in the title of an anonymous and influential fourteenth-century work of Christian spirituality, *The Cloud of Unknowing*.

called *purgation*. This is unknowing just as surely as my students' experiences, but with teeth. It is unknowing turned up to 11. It seems to be a thorough scraping-out of all illusions, a real cleansing of the temple, so to speak. Not content to disassemble your ideas about motion, purgation attacks your fundamental assumptions about God and yourself too. Everything you know—or think you know—about God's love, presence, goodness, compassion, wisdom, etc., is lost. Everything you know—or think you know—about your own identity as worthy or not-so-worthy, as smart or not-so-smart, as daughter or son, as mother or father, as successful or unsuccessful, as Christian or Jewish, etc., is also lost. All labels are torn away. With them go all or nearly all beliefs, including (and perhaps especially) the really good ones. This unknowing called purgation is an inner journey from well-mapped and familiar terrain into a trackless wilderness.

By all accounts it's not a pleasant experience. "When this purgation is most severe, the soul feels very keenly the shadow of death and the lamentations of death and the pains of hell, which consist in feeling itself to be without God, and chastised, and cast out, and unworthy," John wrote.[6] This is disturbing language. Surely there is an element of the pathological here.

Yet the consensus of those who have undergone this radical unknowing is that it happens not when God is absent but when God is so close as to be indiscernible. This is counterintuitive. The living God should not make you feel overshadowed by death. The divine presence should not make you certain of its absence. A God of abundance should not cause you to sense acute loss. Something so good should not make you feel so bad.

Many metaphors seek to describe this paradox, but perhaps the best and simplest is provided by the sun: one who looks directly at the sun will not see light but will be blinded and lost in darkness, and

---

6. John of the Cross, *Dark Night of the Soul* (New York: Image, 1990), 104–5.

this is due not to an absence of light but to its overabundance. Oversaturation by light is, effectively, darkness—but "brilliant darkness."[7] This solar metaphor, due ultimately to Plato, shows up repeatedly in the literature of the Christian mystics.[8] "The more directly we look at the sun, the greater is the darkness which it causes in our visual faculty, overcoming and overwhelming it through its own weakness," John wrote.[9]

Reading through the literature of purgative experiences can be haunting. There are cases of authors who, if they were alive today, would certainly be diagnosed with severe clinical depression. But most of them are not of this variety, and John of the Cross himself drew a clear distinction between spiritual purgation and depression, which he called *melancholia*.[10] Moreover, suffering of itself has no value and true experiences of God are never thoroughly negative—there always comes a lifting of the burden, a dawning of the day, a resurrection. All things are indeed made new, as we shall see.

Purgation via Cosmos

Let us now return to Our Man in Uz.

As we've seen, God is not a pleasant character in the book of Job—it's difficult to warm to a tempest. The whirlwind howls against Job for 125 solid verses, bringing to mind Teresa of Ávila's words:

---

7. The phrase comes from a short but hugely influential treatise called *The Mystical Theology* written by an anonymous sixth-century Syrian monk who has been given the unlikely moniker *Pseudo-Dionysius*.
8. Mystics are those who claim to have had direct experience of God.
9. John of the Cross, *Dark Night of the Soul*, 101.
10. This distinction is not important for the present discussion, but it is described beautifully in Denys Turner's *The Darkness of God: Negativity in Christian Mysticism* (Cambridge: Cambridge University Press, 1998), 226–51.

"Lord, if this is the way you treat your friends, no wonder you have so few of them."[11]

But we might read the vociferous vortex in a more sympathetic light if we interpret Job's experience as a case of purgation via cosmos. Think about it: Job is tormented by his losses and longs for death. Not even sleep offers him respite. "When I say, 'My bed will comfort me, my couch will ease my complaint,' then you scare me with dreams and terrify me with visions so I would choose strangling and death rather than this body," he cries to God in 7:13-15. To all appearances God has abandoned him: "If I go forward, he is not there; or backward, I cannot perceive him" (23:8). His words line up well with John's description of purgation, and for Job it is the cosmos that completes the process.

Purgation is particularly distressing for those who have a major interest in holding onto what is being purged. My students don't have a lot invested in their incorrect assumptions about motion, so they can unknow them and learn basic physics without drama (okay, without *too much* drama). But he who has built his very life on a particular set of beliefs will experience disorientation and even dereliction when these beliefs are disassembled and carted away.

And if ever there was a man who was invested in his beliefs it is Job, who was formed by the standard-issue wisdom of Proverbs. His position at the apex of the social pyramid is sustained by the very model of righteousness that is being challenged first by his experience and ultimately by the vortex. He believes that God is basically himself writ large, so unknowing this divine model brings into question not only his assumptions about God but also those about his own identity. His belief about the centrality of human beings was

---

11. Perhaps apocryphal, but in keeping with Teresa's well-attested wit. Quoted from www.catholicherald.co.uk/commentandblogs/2015/03/28/st-teresa-of-avila-was-a-charming-droll-and-tough-minded-reformer.

also thoroughly deconstructed, leaving him in a brotherly relationship with the dreadful Behemoth (40:15). In the face of these losses, who is he? It's no wonder that Job feels abandoned, homeless, lost in the howling wilderness.

God's unpleasant personality in Job, I propose, is an expression of this pain of purgation, not an objective feature of the divine. The vortex offends not because God is a bully but because, by bringing Job face-to-face with the cosmos, it exposes the gap between what he thought was true and what is actually true. This gap has a name, and it is ignorance. It's not simple ignorance of the "No, Lord, I do not know when the mountain goats give birth" variety. It is the gap, as Job might say, between the hearing of the ear and the seeing of the eye.

An Illumined Cosmos

"I have heard of you by the hearing of the ear, but now my eye sees you," says Job after the cosmic tour is over (42:5).

What had Job heard by the ear? That God was like him but larger, a benevolent and wise patriarch in the sky who valued human beings above all other creatures.

What did Job see with his eye? A God who utterly transcends his old conception and loves the whole cosmos, not just the human part of it.

Yet perhaps Job did not see God at all. What Job *saw* was the earth, the sky, storm clouds, the wilderness, an assortment of strange creatures, and chaos thrashing madly beneath it all. There was no exhibit on the tour called "God." The vortex talked a lot about God, but God was never the object of Job's perception. He saw the cosmos but he claims to have "seen God." How is this possible?

Perhaps the answer lies in this admittedly strange-sounding formula: to "see with the eye" is to see as God sees. In other words, Job did not see God—he was taken up into God's seeing. He "saw God" by seeing the cosmos as God sees it.

"Taken up into God's seeing"—this is strange language. But it is really a simple and concrete matter. A short story, derived from Walker Percy's *Lost in the Cosmos*, illustrates what I mean.

A man is walking in the forest with his young son. The boy sees a bird. Fascinated, he stops and he stares. He whispers, "What is that?" The man looks and says, "That is only a sparrow."

For the man the actual living, breathing, flying creature has been lost behind the label *sparrow*. It has been devalued. In the man's eyes the bird has actually *become* its label. But to the eyes of the boy, who has never before seen a sparrow, the bird is a particular and surprising feature of the living cosmos.

Now, who has perceived the animal and who has not? They both have, of course, but the man has "heard with the ear" while the boy has "seen with the eye." If the man were able to unknow what he knows about "sparrows," he might see the bird as his son does. Its label would fall away and the creature could be recovered in all its unspeakable weirdness.

This unknowing is precisely what happens to Job. It's the gift of purgation: once all concepts and assumptions are deconstructed and hauled away, Job's vision is clear—the log has been removed from his eye, as Jesus might say—and he is able to see the cosmos as God sees it. Before the vortex arrived he was aware of the wilderness creatures but he could not see them. "I am a brother to jackals, and a companion of ostriches," he cries as he bemoans his sorry lot (30:29). He believes his relation to these denizens of desolation exists only by virtue of his miserable circumstances. These animals, in other words, are ugly and embarrassing, just as he is ugly and embarrassing. His vision is blocked. He does not see them; he sees only himself.

But the vortex draws near and the cosmos is illumined. The jackals and ostriches look brand new. He sees that there is nothing shameful about them. He sees that they are beautiful. He sees the mountain goat and the raven and the vulture just as God does: simply and directly, as the free and proud creatures that they are, each one unique and valuable in themselves. They were no longer gamey and embarrassing and bloody dots on the outer fringes of his consciousness, but peculiar and divinely made creatures living within their own communities, communities from which human civilization itself appeared distant and alien.

Empty and Free

"Seeing with the eye" may indeed mean seeing as God sees, but the question of God remains. And that question is: Once purged by the cosmos, what replaces Job's old God-concept?

In one sense that's easy to answer: the God Job gained is not the God Job lost. This new God does not share Job's preoccupation with his own kind. This new God is not a gracious and just patriarch in the sky. This new God is not a local divinity, but attends to business far from, and unrelated to, human civilization. This God loves all things from the modest desert grass to the witless ostrich to the baleful Leviathan. This God is cosmic.

But this God is also inscrutable. In contrast to Ken Ham's God, the God of Job does not lay out everything square and plain. It is clear that the old rules of Proverbs—reward and punishment, if you do good you'll get good, wisdom is the path to prosperity—no longer apply. But nowhere are new rules made clear. They seem to be hidden. God is not straightforward.

This God also seems unpredictable and perhaps even capricious. Back in Chapter 3, I pointed out the preposterous nature of the wager between God and the Accuser and admitted my strong desire to simply write it off. Nevertheless that story remains, grinning up at me out of the pages of the prologue, keeping me guessing: What kind of God does this?

Moreover, it seems that even a God with interests all over the cosmos, who loves all things and balances all needs, etc., still could have done a little more to protect poor Job. God seems to attend more carefully to goats and oxen than to him. Job may not be the most important living thing in the cosmos, but neither is the desert grass. And the losses are not Job's alone—his wife lost ten children. Certainly these children had friends and perhaps their own families. We just can't understand a God who watches over newborn deer but allows such misery to fall upon Job and his family.

The truth is, once the cosmos sweeps out his old God-concept, Job can never understand God again. My physics students' faulty beliefs, once deconstructed, are quickly succeeded by Newton's Laws. These laws are tidy replacements. They neatly fill the conceptual space where the old ideas used to be. But once Job's old ideas about God are purged via cosmos, there is no simple replacement for them. There is no clean conceptual model to fill the space where the old God-as-invisible-patriarch idea used to be. That space remains forever empty and free.

And, judging by Job's response to the cosmic tour, that's how it should be: after losing his idea of God, he walks away from the ash heap with a light step, humbled and relieved and newly open to the world. His old God-concept was heavier baggage than he ever realized.

Ending the Debate

Twice in my life I've had the experience of learning something I already knew. What I mean is, twice in my life I've encountered subjects that were truly new but *felt* old. In both cases I had no idea I had ever considered these subjects in any way, but the shock of recognition indicated otherwise: "I've been thinking this way my whole life!"

The first time was when I took physics as a college sophomore. I had wondered about motion a lot as a kid, but I never realized that *motion* is what I had thought about. So learning physics was like putting on a pair of shoes that were somehow worn and soft in all the right places, like I had been wearing them for years. Yet they were new, right out of the box.

The second time came much later, in seminary. This is when I read the Christian mystics for the first time. And I am completely serious when I say it was not fun, but initially frightening and ultimately liberating. It was like these people—Meister Eckhart, Marguerite Porete, Nicholas of Cusa, Mechtild of Magdeburg, all of whom lived centuries ago—*knew* me. I had read Merton and he had gone deep, but these folks shot straight into the most interior part of me and said something I believed wholeheartedly but, until then, could not verbalize: God is incomprehensible. In God we run up against something altogether beyond even our best thoughts. It sounds simple in the saying, but the recognition of this fact was my theological homecoming.

The difference between God and the cosmos is this: God resists conceptualization and the cosmos does not. The tendency of certain people not to respect this distinction, I believe, is one source of the media spectacle that is the science-versus-religion culture war. On the one hand you have the Ken Hams and Albert Mohlers of the world who think God is capable of being displaced by scientific theories like evolution, and on the other you have scientifically motivated atheists like Richard Dawkins who think the same thing. But one of the lessons of Job is that this assumption is wrong: God is not containable by any concepts, even good ones that last a long time and work fine (until they don't). God is beyond ideas, and essentially so.

Once we let this simple claim settle in, everything changes for Job and for us. He loses his God-concept but gains God, subsequently stepping more lightly as he leaves the ash heap behind. We give up the contemporary assumption of the opposition of science and religion. We can walk away from that debate like Job walked away from his, knowing that it's ultimately no more than an expression of our own desire to control, that is to say deny, God.

And it's hopeful to consider that God is not a manipulable thing, like a chessman or a hammer or a wedge for splitting the world in two. That idea is our own dreadful creation, like making a bomb out of the beauty of physics.

As it is for Job, so it is with us: Only after facing the poverty of even our best ideas about God will we be able to take them lightly, and only then will we be open to seeing God—and the cosmos—as they really are.

# CHAPTER 7

LEARNING TO LOVE LEVIATHAN

Fr. Cavanaugh, back in eleventh-grade philosophy, did more than introduce us to the God of classical theism. He did more than provide proofs and counter-proofs for that particular God's existence. And he did more than give us a guided tour of Western thought. He also asked us a lot of questions. The way he did it cut through the higher philosophical claptrap and jangled our nerves.

It went like this: After a lesson on Aquinas or Kierkegaard or Nietzsche he would pause for a moment, collect his notes, put them away, and begin a slow silent walk around the classroom. Eventually he would stop beside a desk, look into the eyes of the desk's doomed occupant, and ask, in his soft Irish accent, something like, "Susan, do you believe in God?"

"Yes."

"Why?"

Silence. "I don't know."

"Well you need to think about it."

"Okay. I will."

He would remain standing, looking at Susan. After more silence—it felt like an hour—he would add, "Do you believe in God because your mom and dad believe in God?"

Susan would say something, I don't know what. But his point was made: Believing in God because your parents believe in God is not good enough. Believing God loves you because your priest told you God loves you is not good enough. And so on. Fr. Cavanaugh was pretty relentless. "You must have an answer," he would say. Some students got upset. For my part, I was just happy he rarely stopped beside my desk.

There is a sense in which Fr. Cavanaugh might have gone too far. We can't be held individually responsible for every single one of our beliefs. For example: Why do you believe the Earth goes around the Sun? I'm not asking for appeals to authority or to tradition, I'm asking what evidence do *you* have? You almost certainly have none. No experience, no evidence of your senses, no logic guides your conclusion. You believe the Earth goes around the Sun because someone—probably a teacher or parent—told you so, and no one has ever tried to convince you otherwise.

Which is fine. Most of what we believe, we believe because it was told us by someone we trusted. There is nothing wrong with such beliefs. But if we rely too much on that kind of education we might find in the end that we've never learned anything worth knowing. Therefore, when it comes to really important stuff like God, I'm with Fr. Cavanaugh, who, above everything, taught us that all true education is intensely personal.

What We're Actually Talking About

Job would probably agree.

He was a well-educated man. Before his crisis he was a big believer in what he had been taught. But then the bottom dropped out and he began to question his formal education. Why, if the traditional equation of reward-and-punishment were true, would he, the most righteous man in Uz, have suffered so grievously? Conventional theology no longer squared with his experience. In fact, the book of Job can be read as a debate between tradition and personal experience.

Experience cannot teach us all things, but any idea that contradicts experience will, over time, lose its power. Take, for example, one traditional idea that, for me, is fast becoming a relic because it does not accord with experience: creation *ex nihilo* (from nothing).

This idea is simply stated: "God created absolutely everything from absolutely nothing." Creation *ex nihilo* is the primary indicator of God's omnipotence and an integral part of classical theism. The Dogmatic Constitution on the Catholic Faith (which also made an appearance in Chapter 2) puts it this way:

> The one only true God, of His own goodness and almighty power, not for the increase or acquirement of His own happiness, but to manifest His perfection by the blessings which He bestows on creatures, and with absolute freedom of Counsel, created out of nothing, from the very first beginning of time, both the spiritual and the corporeal creature.[1]

In this view the cosmos, including all its creatures, is gratuitous. It does not in any sense add to or subtract from God's blessedness and completeness and distinction and power, for there is not and never has been and never can be any lack in that department: this God is "supremely blessed in and from Himself," and to admit a benefit is to admit a lack. The God of classical theism, in other words, is a standalone God. Ian McFarland, my systematic theology professor, put it this way: "God plus the cosmos is not more than God."

Creatio ex nihilo, "created out of nothing," fits in perfectly with this picture because it underlines not only God's distinction from the cosmos but also God's total power and control over it. God didn't need to create the cosmos but did anyway. God is perfectly free to do so.

---

1. www.ccel.org/ccel/schaff/creeds2.v.ii.i.html.

On a purely intellectual level I get all of this. It is, in its way, appealing. I can even see how it could be true. Although I come down on the liberal side of many questions, my theological reflexes are conservative. I think of tradition as a gift—it is a relief to be given a frame of reference you didn't make up. Plus, as I have confessed, I am a real fan of systems. I love it when complex things fit and work together to make a unified whole.

This explains the great appeal that physics has held for me for nearly thirty years. It also explains my affection for the classical theism I first encountered under Fr. Cavanaugh and explored in much greater detail as an adult in seminary. This theology, like physics, is a fairly integrated set of ideas. Messing with one part (like *ex nihilo*) alters the whole structure. But unlike physics, classical theism appeals to me almost entirely *as a system* and not as a reality that connects meaningfully with the world around me. Lately, when I read things like the Dogmatic Constitution on the Catholic Faith, I pretty quickly find myself asking, Now what is it we're talking about here?

Biblical Chaos

There are alternatives to *ex nihilo*. Some of them are ancient. One of the oldest and most prominent is called *creation from chaos* (I love the name). In this model God created not from nothing but out of a featureless, randomized state of matter and energy called chaos. A good example of this alternative model of creation is found in a very conspicuous place: the first three verses of the Bible.

"In the beginning when God created the heavens and the earth, the earth was a formless void and darkness covered the face of the deep, while a wind from God swept over the face of the waters. Then God said, 'Let there be light'; and there was light" (Genesis 1:1-3). If you read *ex nihilo* here, it's coming from the tradition, not the text. The text itself is a fairly straightforward description of God creating out of a watery and chaotic deep.

This quotation is drawn from the New Revised Standard Version (NRSV). There are other major translations that make creation from chaos impossible to avoid. For example, the Jewish Study Bible (NJPS), a conservative, even scrupulous, translation of one of the oldest biblical manuscripts in existence, puts it this way: "When God began to create heaven and earth—the earth being unformed and void, with darkness over the surface of the deep and a wind from God sweeping over the water—God said, 'Let there be light'; and there was light." We now have a single sentence. The NRSV's second phrase has here become a description of the state of things *when God began to create*. This is clearly inconsistent with *ex nihilo*.

So, was the cosmos created *ex nihilo*? I don't know, but one thing is certain: the Bible wasn't. It was not composed in isolation or in one fell swoop. It did not drop out of the sky fully formed. It evolved, growing slowly out of the culture of ancient Israel and the general milieu of the ancient Near East. In that context "creation" was universally taken to mean "creation from chaos." Genesis 1 is distinct from the creation accounts of ancient Israel's neighbors in many ways, but its description of creation from chaos is not one of them. Whatever Christian tradition eventually came to say about creation, the authors of Genesis knew nothing of *ex nihilo*.

Furthermore, the Bible seems to take creation from chaos for granted in places. Job is one of them. In fact, the climax of God's monologue in chapter 41 is by far the Bible's most extensive treatment of Leviathan, which is, you will recall, the very embodiment of primordial chaos. It is also among the most chaos-friendly passages in scripture. "I will not keep silence concerning its limbs, or its mighty strength, or its splendid frame," God says of the monster (41:12). This unabashed admiration for the chaotic deep stands in contrast to the Israel's fear of the waters and to the trepidation Job felt when he beheld Leviathan. What appears terrible and destructive in human eyes is, from the divine point of view, fertile ground. In the hands of God chaos is transformed from a deadly maelstrom into the foundation of a very good creation.

There are other places in scripture that suggest creation from chaos (e.g., 2 Peter 3:5). On the other hand there are passages that may be understood to support *ex nihilo* (e.g., Hebrews 11:3, Colossians 1:16, and Romans 4:17). But on neither side does one find a single unambiguous statement.[2]

Genesis describes creation from chaos and the Bible in general is noncommittal, which makes one wonder why classical Christianity so clearly favors *ex nihilo*. This preference has to do with certain debates that occurred between the early church and a number of influential schools of ancient philosophy. The details of these debates, which occurred mostly in the second century, are not of interest here. It suffices only to say that, at the time, there seem to have been perfectly good reasons for establishing creation from nothing as the standard view.

But there is no reason, outside of tradition, to insist on *ex nihilo*. Obviously this is not a sufficient reason to reject it, but we've learned from Job that tradition alone is not sufficient warrant for retaining a doctrine. Bildad, reproving Job for his decidedly nontraditional and nearly blasphemous words, says to him, "For inquire now of bygone generations, and consider what your ancestors have found. Will they not teach you and utter words out of their understanding?" (8:8, 10). Apparently they will not—Bildad is later upbraided by God for not speaking rightly (42:8).

It was experience that pushed Job to reject tradition, and experience leads me to question *ex nihilo*. Two kinds of experience work together to do this: scientific and personal.

---

2. For Catholic and Orthodox believers the Apocrypha only heightens the ambiguity. The Bible's most explicit statements on both sides of the question are found here: 2 Maccabees 7:28 in favor of *ex nihilo* and Wisdom 11:17 against.

The Big Bang. Therefore God!

The cosmos, like the Bible, is not overtly friendly to creation *ex nihilo*. Or, to put it another way, scientific experience does not support the doctrine.

Many will stop me right there, citing the Big Bang theory, which looks a lot like *ex nihilo*. Take Pope Pius XII: "With that concreteness which is characteristic of physical proofs, [science] has confirmed the contingency of the universe and also the well-founded deduction as to the epoch when the cosmos came forth from the hands of the Creator. Hence, creation took place in time. Therefore, there is a Creator. Therefore, God exists!"[3]

Thus spoke the pope in his 1951 address to the Pontifical Academy of Sciences. As confident as these words sound, he misstated the scientific consensus regarding the Big Bang—some scientists liked it and others did not.

In any case, it was not just theologians who saw religious significance to the Big Bang. Scientists also got their words in. The British astronomer Fred Hoyle, who coined the phrase "Big Bang," was vehemently opposed to the theory, and his opposition had as much to do with religion as science. He thought it made natural history seem too much like "a story." He believed it imported "religious ideas" into science and even took some of his fellow scientists to task over their gullibility to such ideas, claiming in a 1949 BBC broadcast that "the reason why scientists like the Big Bang is because they are overshadowed by the book of Genesis. It is deep within the psyche of most scientists to believe in the first page of Genesis."[4]

Neither the pope nor Hoyle was completely out to lunch. On the face of it the Big Bang theory does seem to support *ex nihilo*. The standard interpretation of the theory says that not only stuff,

---

3. www.papalencyclicals.net/Pius12/P12EXIST.HTM
4.www.bbc.co.uk/blogs/adamcurtis/entries/512cde83-3afb-3048-9ece-dba774b10f89

but also space and time themselves were created at the instant of the Big Bang, at which time the cosmos was in a state known as a *singularity*. In this view there was no space and no time, indeed, there was *nothing at all* (whatever that might mean) until the Big Bang. The singularity appeared not in space and time—space and time appeared in the singularity. The cosmos itself came out of nothing whatsoever.

But we should not be too quick to draw this conclusion, because it's not demanded by science. When we look far back in time, we find a breakdown of physical law before we get to the singularity. In the same way that there's a limit to how far away in space we can see, there's a limit to how far back in time we can "see." There is a kind of wall in time and we cannot investigate the state of the cosmos on the early side of that wall, which sits a tiny fraction of a second on this side of the singularity.[5] We do not know what happened before that time. The cosmos may have existed before that moment in a number of different forms: contracting, oscillating, or some other configuration. It may be infinitely old and it may not be. Scientifically speaking that is not known. On the question "what happened before the Big Bang?" science, strictly speaking, remains agnostic.

Out of Chaos, a New (Gradual, Continuous, Open-Ended) Thing

Others will have theological objections to my claim that scientific experience is not particularly friendly to creation from nothing.

Creation ex nihilo, they say, is a theological idea, while *the cosmos* is a scientific one. The two do not overlap, and one cannot explain the other. In particular, science, which is about change and process

---

5. That is, it cannot be investigated until physicists develop a workable theory of quantum gravity. Which may be a while.

within the cosmos, can neither support nor rule out *ex nihilo*, which is about God's relation *to* the cosmos. In this view creation is not about any particular event (or events). Rather, it is about God's sustenance and governance of all things in all places and at all times. It has nothing to do with the specific nature of physical reality. "Creation is the radical causing of the whole existence of whatever exists," writes William E. Carroll. "Theories in the natural sciences account for change . . . [in contrast,] creation accounts for the existence of things, not for changes in things."[6] Carroll is sticking closely to Aquinas, and he represents classical theism well.

Again I feel the gravity of tradition, but I can't get past my insistence, and it doesn't seem too much to ask, that both the theological idea of creation and the character of God have *something* to do with the nature of physical reality. There is a precedent for this kind of thinking: In the High Middle Ages Aquinas and Dante and others saw a match between the God of classical theism and the (unbiblical) cosmos of Aristotle. The words of Whitehead are worth repeating: "Whatever suggests a cosmos, suggests a religion."

And since the specific nature of all physical reality (and not just of life) can be expressed accurately by the single word *evolving*, we seek models of creation and of God that connect with this predominant aspect of the cosmos.

It seems to me that the ancient idea of creation from chaos should be translated into a new image of creation as *gradual, continuous, and open-ended*. This is the cosmos that I know and love—it appears to be more like a tree growing from the dirt than a rabbit pulled from a hat. The tree is an image of order being drawn out of chaos, and I see that every day, all around me and *in* me; everything good emerges from something else, organized or not. The magic

---

6. www.firstthings.com/article/1999/11/aquinas-and-the-big-bang, FT #97, Nov. 99, 18–20.

trick representing *ex nihilo* is something I have no experience with, around me or within me.

Everything good comes out of something else, organized or not. Maybe the Greeks were right: from nothing comes nothing.

God works with what is at hand, and what is at hand is often chaos. We don't know exactly how the ancients imagined chaos, but we might reimagine it as unformed and randomized matter and energy. A good example is the early cosmos: it was uniform (that is, there were no clumps), it was the same temperature everywhere, and its particles moved in random directions.[7] If it had been sound, it would have been white noise. Out of this noise emerged the stars and planets, *T. rex*, Akron, Ohio, Albert Einstein, and the Chia Pet. Order from chaos, indeed.

And God works cooperatively. God does not stand wholly apart from creation, does not reach in and coerce it. Creation occurs only with the participation of the cosmos (including its creatures) and never overpowers it. Creation occurs always out of creation. Creation did not happen in the past any more than it is happening now. A new thing is always being made.[8]

This resonates with a cosmos in which both structure and creatures emerge slowly. It makes theological sense of that timeline my dad showed me when I was a child. It makes sense out of the billions of years of evolution, of the seeming randomness of so many things, and of the arbitrariness of suffering. Since God cannot act in opposition to the raw material of the cosmos, God is not in absolute control of all things. Kittens are sometimes born with two faces; mass extinctions do occur; all people, even the righteous, suffer.

---

7. These things were not strictly, mathematically true of the early cosmos. If they had been we would not be here.
8. Some will see process theology in what I am here proposing. While I am influenced by that school of thought, I do not see myself as a process theologian, for I do not subscribe to it in its full philosophical form.

A Matter of Holes

"One's theology is largely a matter of what holes one can live with," a wise friend once told me. There are several reasons why *ex nihilo* might be such a hole. One reason is social: By placing God in a position of separateness and omnipotence—recall Dante's God enthroned high above all things—*ex nihilo* suggests a theology of empire, of concentrated and unilateral absolute power. This certainly played well in the fourteenth century but fails to ring true in modern ears. Another reason is psychological: At times I suspect that *ex nihilo* is less about God's nature and more about what we human beings most desperately want—control. In other words, I have moments when the God of classical theism seems like little more than ego projection on a cosmic scale. A third reason one might want to reject *ex nihilo* is conceptual: It's just not possible to conceive of the absolute nothingness—no space, no time—out of which the cosmos was made.

Ultimately, though, I can live with these holes. For me they're not truly problematic. But there are others I can't live with. One of them is that *ex nihilo*, and indeed the God of classical theism, does not connect with me or my life or any actualities that I know. Not that everything is about me and my life (one of the lessons I have drawn from Job is that, in fact, very little is about me and my life), but there comes a time when one must look in the mirror and ask, with that sage Dr. Phil, "How's that working for you?" And the truth is, *ex nihilo* and the God of classical theism no longer work for me at all. At no point in my actual three-dimensional life do these ideas connect. Outside the system of classical theism I carry around in my head, creation from nothing carries no meaning and produces no fruit.

A Nightmare in Midtown

My trouble with *ex nihilo* started when I was about eight years old. A few years earlier my parents had divorced and Mom had returned to her native habitat: the city. After the dust settled we kids began a routine of visiting her every Sunday. The visits took place in the afternoon between morning and evening church services.

Midtown Atlanta afforded exposure to things that suburbia, by its very design and to its obvious success, did not. I'm not referring to fineries such as museums and symphonies and architecture but to actual life, which is not, in general, decorous. Screeching and groaning public transportation, hulking buildings, and people, so many people, filled my Sunday afternoons. For me the city was new races and stripes of human beings: the wretchedly poor, the extravagantly rich, loud people, silent people, stoned people. It was during these visits that Mom taught me the finer points of her favorite hobby—people watching. We would sit on the bench in Piedmont Park and make up stories about the characters walking past. The parade was unceasing. Overall I savored the spectacle of actual life. But one Sunday it showed up in its extreme tragic mode, openly and without apology.

Mom drove a white 1963 Ford Falcon. We piled in it so she could take us back to church up in shiny Buckhead, where we would get our evening's dose of Jesus and Baptist Fellowship before returning home for another week of routine. I rode in the back seat. We approached a red light at Piedmont Avenue and slowed. The Falcon stopped, the first car at the light.

Mom suddenly turned her head to the right. "What's going on?" she said.

Northbound traffic on Piedmont had abruptly halted, as had all pedestrians in view. They were strangely still and their gazes converged on a point just beyond the first stopped car, about ten feet in front of the Falcon's front bumper and four car lengths to the right. No one spoke and no one moved. We could not see what they saw for all the people and cars about.

Then we did. Out of the silent group on our right emerged a woman. She was limping and her face was distorted with grief and fear and rage, all three. Never had I seen such an expression, and I hope never to again. All eyes followed her. A man ran up to her and grabbed her shoulders, urgently saying something to her. She pushed him away. He tried again. Again he was put off. He let her go.

She was limping as she crossed the street directly in front of us. Her body convulsed with sobs. She remounted the sidewalk and tottered south toward Downtown, alone. "What's wrong with her?" my brother Dan asked.

The light changed. Northbound traffic resumed and we turned right and moved with it. But the woman's face had sounded an alarm in me. At the time seatbelts were optional, so I turned with my knees on the seat and rested my chin on my forearms under the sloping rear window. I watched her through it as we accelerated away from her.

Therefore I was the only one in the car who saw her step, with obvious intention, off the sidewalk and into the path of an onrushing city bus. It struck her and she was pitched violently onto the streets of Atlanta.

This time she did not walk away, limping or otherwise. The Falcon followed Piedmont around a bend, and the scene was fixed that way in my memory.

Two hours later I was sitting with my family in a pew near the front of the sanctuary. The evening service was drawing to a close. William Self, our pastor, stood in the pulpit above us. The lights had been extinguished save one or two filtered spots that shone on him and made the scene appear airbrushed and gauzy in a very 1970s kind of way. The organ exhaled stanza after stanza of "Turn Your Eyes Upon Jesus."

I knew what would happen next because it happened every Sunday night. Its power was in the way it marked the week's passage with gentleness and hope. Without a trace of hurry Dr. Self reached out and grasped the edges of the large pulpit. He tipped himself forward, smiled, and scanned the congregation. Back and forth. It was very dramatic. Then he rocked back on his heels, paused, and said what he always said: "It's been a good day."

He then executed the remainder of the formula: A theological, item-by-item analysis of why that particular day had been a good one. It lasted no more than five minutes and was capped off by that most revered of Baptist traditions, the invitation. It all added up to a single undeniable message: We could feel good now because we had made it through another week and were once again safe in God's great house.

It's been nearly forty years since that Sunday, and I still remember thinking that it *would* have been a good day if God had stopped that woman from jumping in front of that bus. I actually imagined a big invisible hand reaching down and walling her off from the street.

A God who creates gratuitously, *ex nihilo*, and who is in no way constrained or limited by that creation, must retain all power. This is essential to the God of classical theism. Yet apparently this same God chooses freely to not exercise that power, overtly or otherwise, to prevent such nightmares as the one I witnessed that day in Midtown.

This is my problem with *ex nihilo*, and by extension, the God of classical theism. This is the hole I cannot live with.

A Faith That Works

There is another.

I have longed for God my whole life. In this I am no different than any other human being. But for me the search for God has been very close to the surface, both explicit and obvious. It has also been churchy. Since I was a child I have loved being in sanctuaries and chapels. As a graduate student and professor I've sought out places of worship on whatever campus I happened to be, usually in solitude. I find solace in such places. When I was young I loved Sunday evening services especially, even after the tragedy in Midtown. As a high school senior I preached on Youth Sunday. I was ambivalent about that assignment. On one hand I was just beginning to question Christianity and I felt a little weird about standing in the pulpit and talking about Jesus, but on the other it felt exactly like home.

It was my longing for God that drove my questioning. Later my longing took me away from the faith, drew me toward science, and then brought me back to the fold, science in hand. It was my longing for God that led me to be active in church after church during my late twenties and thirties, and to leave a tenured faculty position for seminary when I was forty. It was my longing for God that led me to be ordained in 2014.

But for more of these years than I care to admit, the more I longed for God the more distant God seemed. I struggled, as so many do, with depression and addiction. Living seemed pointless much of the time. For a couple of years not a day went by that I did not think about how pleasant it would be to die. At times these thoughts were nearly constant, persistent evil whispers in the back of my head. The battle continued for some time, even after I joined a recovery group and began working the steps of the program, even after I admitted my powerlessness and reached out (again) to God.

Slowly I was able to relax and allow God to work on me, and today things are better. I have been clean for years and haven't been depressed or considered suicide for longer than that. (Without recovery I could not be writing this book.)

One of the hardest parts of the process had to do with my God-concept. I have spent most of my life ruled by my head, but in order to recover I had to abandon *every single idea* I had ever had about God, except for one: God loves me and wants me to be better. Everything else had to go. Something like this happens for all addicts in recovery, but for me the deconstruction had to be complete because my opinions about God were both definite and unhelpful: I believed God was separate, distinct, and essentially unrelated to the cosmos and the things in it, including me; I believed God had created the cosmos *ex nihilo* and therefore had the power to reach down and fix me without my having very much to do with it; I believed God lived *up there*. In short, I believed in an abstraction. And it is not possible to be healed by an abstraction.

I don't know how *ex nihilo* works for anyone else, but for me that doctrine, along with the God of classical theism it is so closely bound up with, no longer works at all. Experience, both scientific and personal, has trumped it. Classical theism may make sense for others but for me it's poison, especially in its more abstract and rarified forms.

Meanwhile the idea of God creating from chaos has been extremely helpful. It leads me toward a faith that works. It brings God down into the mess of my life; it makes it possible for every place to be a holy place; it helps me understand how God can, seemingly without effort, channel the chaos of my life, which seems so deadly and destructive and monstrous to me, into a new and living creation.

For one who is scientifically trained, it's radically hopeful to think that life—my life, my family's life, my recovery, even my writing of this book—is not *like* creation, but *is* creation, and in the fullest theological sense of the word. Creation from chaos makes God present not only in the most distant reaches of the cosmos but in my one tiny and particular human life. It tells me I belong, a small but real part of all things, no longer lost in the cosmos.

CHAPTER 8

JESUS EVOLVES

For us as well as for Job, the cosmos rules out certain God-concepts and encourages others. This also applies, it turns out, to our ideas of Jesus.

Jesus, Keepin' It Positive

If you want to understand Jesus, start with the Last Son of Krypton.

Primary and secondary state schools in England offer religion as an academic subject. Religious Education courses are not compulsory, but many students enroll in them in order to understand the cultural significance not only of Christianity but of other faith traditions. The number of Englanders who regularly attend worship is low and getting lower, however, so more and more children have little to no knowledge of major religious figures and stories. Therefore about ten years ago some educators turned to movies and comic book characters for help: *The Matrix* is useful for demonstrating the Buddhist idea of *maya*, illusion; Darth Vader is a universally recognized symbol of evil; Harry Potter makes a decent Moses figure. And, when it came to introducing Jesus to young people, educators looked to the Man of Steel.

> Superman is going to be used by religious education teachers to help youngsters to understand the concept of Jesus Christ. Children will be told that Superman is like Jesus because both

arrived on Earth after being sent here by their fathers, both moved from relative obscurity as children to greater prominence, both help the people with whom they were sent to live and both stand up for truth against injustice and evil.[1]

I'm not surprised by the choice. My experience is that many believers really do think of Jesus as superhuman. For instance, several weeks ago I was in a Bible study with a bunch of friends. We were discussing the first chapter of Mark, a book that cuts to the chase. The first twenty verses contain Jesus' baptism, his sojourn in the wilderness, and his calling of the disciples Simon, Andrew, James, and John.

As the discussion developed, a question arose concerning Jesus' self-knowledge: How much did he know about his mission, and when did he know it? It was suggested (by me) that he didn't completely comprehend his calling until just before he started his ministry. Maybe he was a little vague about it even at his baptism and it was the wilderness experience that clarified things for him (as it did for Job, the Israelites, John the Baptist, etc.). This idea brought concern to the faces of several folks, one of whom suggested this theory takes away from Jesus' divinity: Jesus was God, so he must have known everything, including what his mission was, from the get-go.

A similar concern was raised in an earlier meeting. At issue then was the nature of Jesus' relationship with John the Baptist. The idea was floated that John had been Jesus' mentor. Biblically and historically, there's no direct evidence for this, but Jesus and John had likely developed an intimate connection by the time Jesus' ministry began. At one point Jesus calls John "the greatest of those born of women" (e.g., Matthew 11:11) and is later profoundly grieved upon his death (Matthew 14:13). So the idea that John and Jesus

---

1. www.thetimes.co.uk/tto/news/uk/article1948574.ece.

had a mentor-mentee relationship, while not certain, is plausible. But again several folks asked: Why would Jesus, who was God, need a mentor?

Most memorable, however, is a discussion I had with a close friend many years ago. It was Holy Week and we were talking about Jesus' passion. Matthew's and Mark's account of Jesus' crucifixion came up. In those books his last words from the cross are, "My God, my God, why have you forsaken me?" I suggested that Jesus actually experienced God's abandonment, that he really and truly, as much as any person who has ever walked the earth, at that moment ceased to believe in God's good care and providence.

My friend would have none of it. He said, "No, he was just quoting Psalm 22:1."

Which is true. That psalm is a lamentation of one who is dehumanized and mocked by his enemies. So I agreed, but asked why that psalm in particular came to Jesus' mind as he faced death. Could he not have chosen another?

"Maybe," my friend said, "but you know how the psalm ends, don't you?"

"No," I admitted, "I don't."

"It ends in praise," he said. "Jesus chose his words carefully. He knew that everyone who heard them would know how that psalm ends. He was saying, in effect, 'everything's bad now but things are going to work out. It's cool. It'll be okay.'"

Introducing Hovercraft Jesus

These stories do not, in the strict sense, prove anything about how people in general view Jesus. Or, as we like to say in the sciences, the plural of "anecdote" is not "proof." Nonetheless I think they point to a very real assumption shared by very many Christians: under his human skin, Jesus was essentially superhuman.

It's not hard to make such a case. Despite the terrible things that happen to him, Jesus often comes across as authoritative and totally in-control. As a twelve-year-old he has enough knowledge—and chutzpah—to teach in the Temple. As an adult he runs intellectual circles around the scribes and Pharisees without breaking a sweat. There are places where he seems to communicate wordlessly through some alternate dimension with demons and other spirits. He reads minds and knows things about people he's never met. He has power over the chaotic cosmos. His body holds healing power. And then, of course, Jesus heals and multiplies loaves and fishes and walks on water. He keeps his cool while on trial, and after the resurrection he walks through walls, disappears occasionally, and, in a final show of otherworldliness, rises into heaven.

It seems that such a savior could not possibly be unsure of his mission. He seems to not need help, and he doesn't get it. The apostles do some good work post-Pentecost, but they're not exactly a competent crew while Jesus walks the earth. He pretty much has to push through alone (which may not have been so hard for him, since he was God). This Jesus is a self-sufficient and fully autonomous savior.

Even Gethsemane does not seem to deter people who want to believe in a superhuman Jesus. More than once I've had conversations with fellow Christians who seem to think that yes, Jesus got a little anxious there in the garden, but he never really doubted the outcome. He knew the plan. He *knew*, even as the disciples denied him, betrayed him, failed to keep watch, and finally broke and ran, that he would be back.

This Jesus is indeed a lot like Superman: he's an alien, an immigrant from an unearthly realm sent to us—yes, by his father—from the heavens. He looks like one of us but is not *really* one of us. Like Clark Kent, his humble exterior is merely a cover for out-of-this-world powers. He's essentially distinct from the general run of earthly creatures. He is the Messiah of Steel. My New Testament professor,

Luke Timothy Johnson, had a funny name for this all-knowing, mind-reading, levitating, seemingly magical savior: *Hovercraft Jesus.*

Of course, the Gospels do not fully accord with Hovercraft Jesus. In them Jesus comes across as a regular guy as often as not. He connects easily and directly with ordinary people. He is always eating and drinking with friends. He loves children. He weeps. He mourns. He expresses anger. He gets prickly with his mom. He tries to escape the crowds that ceaselessly hound him. He sweats blood. And, he dies.

But many contemporary Christians seem to think this is an act, a cover for the hovercraft within. In this view Jesus' weeping and laughing and drinking is Jesus in Clark Kent mode, biding his time and watching for trouble: a storm on the sea, a leper, a party without wine, a woman with dropsy. These situations allow him to do all the mind-blowing stuff he *really* came here for. The hovercraft version of Jesus' humanity, in other words, is incidental, not essential, to his identity.

Obsolete Cosmos, Obsolete God, Obsolete Jesus

It's not hard to understand the appeal of Hovercraft Jesus: he knows all things and we do not, he is in control and we are not, he has all power and we do not. And these things—knowledge, control, power—are what we really want. In this way Hovercraft Jesus, like the God of classical theism, sometimes seems like little more than ego-projection.

It's also not hard to figure out where Hovercraft Jesus came from: Up There. He is the emissary of the God of classical theism. If God is, as the First Vatican Council put it, "Almighty, Eternal, Immense, Incomprehensible, Infinite in intelligence, in will, and in all perfection" and is "really and essentially distinct from the world, of supreme blessedness in and from Himself, and ineffably exalted above all things which exist, or are conceivable, except Himself," and if Jesus is God, then Jesus too is all of these things.

Hovercraft Jesus, like the God of classical theism who sent him down from heaven, is at home in the obsolete cosmos.

Recall that cosmos, divided as it is into two distinct regions: down here below the moon where change, death, corruption, and decay rule, and up there above the moon where all is calm and orderly and changeless and divine. Down here the elements of earth, water, air, and fire mix in a perpetual stew and the human race slogs it out amid the general blight; up there heaven abides like divinity itself, pure and unknowable. The boundary between these realms is real and physical. It's clearly marked, permanent, and, short of death, impassable. Not like a wall dividing two nations on earth, it marks the lower boundary of a realm qualitatively distinct in every way from the one we inhabit. And, beyond it all, at the summit of all things seen and unseen, the almighty God of classical theism is perched, further above the stars than the stars are above us.

How does Jesus fit into this cosmic zoning scheme? The Nicene Creed, one of the founding documents of classical theism, suggests an answer:

> [The] Lord Jesus Christ, the Only Begotten Son of God, born of the Father before all ages, God from God, Light from Light, true God from true God, begotten, not made, consubstantial with the Father; through him all things were made. For us men and for our salvation he came down from heaven, and by the Holy Spirit was incarnate of the Virgin Mary, and became man.[2]

There it is: Jesus "came down from heaven," or, as the author of Hebrews put it, "passed through the heavens" (Hebrews 4:14) on his way to us. Hovercraft Jesus—all-knowing, all-seeing, all-powerful,

---

2. The Nicene Creed was established a thousand years before the medieval cosmos reached its highest stage of development. Much of that development was influenced by Nicene theology.

essentially distinct—seems inevitable in light of this creed and the centuries of theology and tradition it has inspired.

When this Jesus came down, he brought the God of Dante's cosmos with him. He was like a divine spark on the ash heap of humanity, absolutely exceptional amid the muck of earthly life. He may have looked like us and in some ways acted like us, but he was not like us. He was a different kind of being from a different kind of place and possessed powers and knowledge appropriate to that place and to the God that resides there. (This notion has survived—and even thrived—despite the doctrine, established nearly 1,600 years ago and only a century or so after the Nicene Creed, which says that Jesus was simultaneously divine *and* human, "truly God and truly man."[3])

Hovercraft Jesus is as static as the obsolete cosmos in which he resides. Like that cosmos, he exhibits no true development or maturation. Though he outwardly exhibits all the stages of normal human development, this is only part of his Clark Kent act. In reality he arrives on earth with everything he needs to save the world: all the knowledge and power of the God of Up There. In such a scenario, there is no need—or room—for growth. Therefore those who advocate for Hovercraft Jesus feel discomfort upon the suggestion that Jesus was ever unclear about his mission or needed a mentor.

Regular-Person Things

In an evolving cosmos, Jesus evolves.

He *was* fully human, after all. Therefore he had to learn as we learn and grow as we grow. Like ours, his understanding of himself, the cosmos, and his role in it arose gradually, and perhaps fitfully. As a child he probably looked and acted much like his peers.

---

3. Quote drawn from the Confession of Chalcedon. This understanding of the Incarnation, like the doctrine of the Trinity, was developed by councils of the Roman Catholic Church. However, they are authoritative for the vast majority of Protestants and, in slightly altered forms, for Orthodox believers as well.

He clearly understood his religion early—he *was* teaching in the Temple as a boy—but as far as his identity and his understanding of his mission go, I believe these things dawned on him gradually. A slowly developing identity makes sense to me because it is at home in the evolving cosmos and because it accords with experience. So much of an individual human life is driven by the quest for self-knowledge, it seems impossible to imagine any truly human life without it.

Yet he was "without sin" (Hebrews 4:15). How could he have developed as we do, with all the difficulty, back-stepping, and pain it entails, without sinning? I don't know, but so often we claim this formula and move along without ever questioning our deeper assumptions about what sin looks like (and therefore about Jesus himself). Some things, we might agree, are obviously sinful: character assassination, taking advantage of others' weaknesses, turning one's back on one's fellows in their time of need. These things are not only not-divine; they are, in a word, inhuman. Engaging in them dehumanizes us.

But what about less obvious cases? Does sin look like doing regular things regular people do every day? For example, does sin look like making mistakes? Maybe not. Maybe Jesus made mistakes. Maybe he sometimes called acquaintances by the wrong name. Maybe he occasionally forgot appointments. Maybe his grades weren't uniformly excellent. Was he a pain in the ass to his parents? Did he go through moody phases? Oversleep? Procrastinate? Did he have any annoying habits? Did he enjoy practical jokes a little too much? Did he ever get drunk, even once, even a little? Did he ever win a bet and feel good about it?

For many the answer will be a self-evident No. The notion that Jesus was ever annoying, wrong, or intemperate brings him a little too low, some will say, and makes him ungodly, too much like us.

If these questions offend, it may be because of the near-complete triumph of Hovercraft Jesus over the popular imagination. This Jesus, due to his supreme knowledge and total control, would have always known everyone's name, made perfect grades, woken up on time, obeyed his parents, etc.

In order to accept Hovercraft Jesus we must believe that humanity and divinity are necessarily mutually opposed to one another, just as they were in the medieval cosmos. Down here beneath the moon are absent-mindedness, poor grades, weakness, overenthusiasm, and insecurity. Arrayed against these things are perpetual and absolute presence of mind, infinite knowledge and power, total control, and complete certainty. These are heavenly, and Hovercraft Jesus, in crossing the boundary between heaven and earth, brings them to us, wrapped in the garment of human flesh.

If Jesus was ever a genuine pain in the ass to his parents it might threaten this division between heaven and earth because it suggests that he might not have always been "infinite in the perfection of love." And beings that are all-powerful and "infinite in intelligence" don't forget people's names or do poorly on exams. If Jesus is "of supreme blessedness in and from himself," he would never seek the pleasure of mild drunkenness.

I do not insist that Jesus did every single regular-person thing I can imagine. My point is not that he had any particular foible or quirk or limitation. My concern is with a Jesus, who, over the course of three-plus decades on earth, never did *any* regular-person things at all. Because such a Jesus is not actually human. Such a Jesus is at once unbelievable and dull. Hovercraft Jesus is so far removed from anything I can even vaguely relate to or even *hope* to relate to, so unearthly and so unlovable, and so contrary to experience, that I can hardly even work up the energy to pretend to be interested in him.

The Wall That Isn't

The old cosmic division between the earth and the heavens, which dominated Western philosophy and science for nearly 2,000 years, *does not exist*. It was a construct of our imaginations and nothing more. You probably knew that. But you may be surprised to learn, how terribly important its absence has turned out to be. The truth is, if it had been there, we would not be here. We owe our lives to the wall that isn't.

In way of explanation, I'd like you to consider your hand. Look at it. Either hand will do.

You see folds and wrinkles and, if you look more closely, tiny furrows and plateaus. If you were to look through a decent microscope at the feature of the cosmos you call your hand, you would see that, up close, it looks altogether alien, like a bizarre mountainous landscape. Peering deeper you would encounter individual cells, then large molecules such as DNA and finally small molecules such as water—there's a lot of water in your hand.

We could go deeper—there are plenty of layers yet—but it's here that I want to stop and ask: Where did that water molecule come from? Where did the oxygen atom come from, where did the two hydrogen atoms come from, and how did they come to be stuck to the oxygen, looking for all the world like Mickey Mouse's ears on his round mouse head?

Well, it started a long time ago in a galaxy not too far away (as galaxies go).

The hydrogens, it turns out, are primordial, having been formed just after the Big Bang.[4] Pretty much no hydrogen has been made since. All the hydrogen atoms in the cosmos are about 13.8 billion years old. The ones in your hand's water molecule are no exception.

---

4. 300,000 years after the big bang, actually. This may seem like a long time but if you compare it to the age of the cosmos it's like comparing ten minutes to a year.

They drifted about the cosmos as individuals for at least 100 million years and probably much, much longer before they found themselves stuck to your oxygen.

And how did *that* happen? I'll tell you, but first we need to consider the origin of that oxygen atom. It's of a younger generation than the hydrogens, having been formed in the core of some massive star long after your hydrogens made the scene, and probably at some location far from them. That's right, stars slow-cook elements like gigantic spherical crockpots. Your oxygen atom was formed in a star and was blown out into the cosmos when the star reached the end of its life. Afterward it drifted hither and thither for some incomprehensible amount of time before it met up with the hydrogens.

That meeting probably happened something like this: several hundred million years if not billions of years after the oxygen atom was blown into space, it and the two hydrogens wound up in the same cloud of gas.[5] Then, like three perfect strangers walking down the very same street on the very same day, they found themselves momentarily shoulder-to-shoulder. Just as they came within speaking distance and were set to move on, never to see one another again, a not-very-unusual thing happened nearby, a star was born. When that star's nuclear engine switched on it sent shock waves of heat and light through the cloud, and our three atoms were pushed together in a single beautiful stroke. They stuck fast and have been traveling together ever since, which has also been a while: probably between 5 and 10 billion years.

No one can say where that molecule has been in that time. One thing is for sure, though: several billions of years ago it found itself caught up in the cloud that was to give birth to the solar system. It didn't fall into the center of the cloud where the sun formed, nor did it get tossed out into the cold dark periphery. Instead it settled

---

5. There are *lots* of gas clouds in the cosmos; Google "M42" to see one of the most famous—and lovely.

somewhere in the middle and became part of what was to eventually be the sun's third planet, our home.[6]

It has moved around the Earth ceaselessly ever since. It may have been expelled into the atmosphere by a volcano long before life showed up. It has been part of oceans that don't exist anymore and has been down rivers unseen by human eyes, or *any* eyes for that matter. Your molecule was certainly a regular participant in the rain that fell on the dinosaurs during their 165-million-year rule of the planet. It may have even been part of a dinosaur. It probably at least passed through one. And if that particular water molecule didn't, lots of others in your hand did.

And, sometime between ten years ago and just now, that same water molecule became part of you. It won't be part of you for long, and neither will any of the other zillions of water molecules that make up the majority of your weight.

Every atom and molecule in your body—and in the earth— could tell a similar story.

Imagine a house made of bricks, boards, wiring, switches, nails, fuses, sheets of drywall, and shingles. Now imagine that, over the course of ten years, piece by piece, every brick, board, wire, switch, nail, fuse, sheet of drywall, and shingle is replaced by an exact duplicate. Imagine that this keeps happening for years, one full turnover occurring every decade or so. In the end it's the same house, right? Or is it? Or is what we call "the house" more like a pattern into which things come to fit for a while, only to be replaced and sent on their way? Either way, your body is like that house.

You are made of things that existed long before you were conceived and that will continue to exist long after you pass away. They

---

6. A leading theory says that much of the earth's water came from comets, which are made largely of ice and which used to strike the earth regularly. Comets are part of the solar system and were formed at the same time as the sun and planets, and they arose out of the same gas cloud as the sun and planets.

are teamed up to make you right now—and I do mean right now. Many of them are on the way out as you read. Others are just arriving. These atoms don't know they're part of you. They're just atoms. They're not even alive. But you are.

I don't know what qualifies as an official miracle, but this seems like one to me: the most remote reaches of the cosmos are so close to us as to *be* us. We may have been formed from the dust of the ground, but the dust of the ground is star-stuff, prepared billions of years ago among the swirling lights of heaven.

Human (Like Jesus)

Jesus is like the cosmos.

In the cosmos there is no distinction between the earth and the heavens. These two realms are really and absolutely one. In Jesus there is also no distinction. He challenges our insistence on separating humanity from divinity, just as science challenged our insistence on separating the earth—indeed, our very flesh and bones—from the heavens.

The evolving cosmos suggests that, in our desire to keep them separate, we have misunderstood both heaven and earth, and with them divinity and humanity. Perhaps divinity does not mean knowing everything, or having all power, or being distinct from other creatures. Maybe it doesn't mean not making mistakes or having no limits. Maybe divinity is closer and less spectacular than we think.

Hovercraft Jesus—all-knowing, totally in control, omnipotent, and, in the end, utterly alien—is a fantasy we've cooked up because we don't want to be human (like Jesus). In other words, we have made Jesus more than we can possibly be so we don't have to become who we can possibly be. By setting up a superhuman Jesus—a Jesus who has infinite knowledge and infinite power and who has zero foibles, zero off-putting quirks, and never once does a single regular-person thing like forgetting an appointment or oversleeping—we deny our-selves the possibility of becoming anything like him. That's hard to do, and that's why we don't want to do it—but that is exactly what he calls us to do.

One of the great moments of my life came when I understood for the first time that being a Christian is about one thing and one thing only: making a conscious commitment to follow Jesus. "Fol-low me"—that's what Jesus asked of his disciples; that's what he asked of Mary Magdalene; that's what he asked of the rich young ruler, and that's what he asks of us. He did not ask us to accept cer-tain statements about him and reject others, or to identify with a cer-tain denomination or church, or to work for particular causes or to favor a certain Bible translation. These things may come, and many of them are important, but doing them or not doing them does not make one a Christian or a non-Christian.

But following or not following Jesus does. To follow Jesus is to allow yourself to become like him in whom there is no distinction. It is, step by tiny step, to lose the distinction in yourself. To follow him, you must trust him the way he trusts God. It means surrendering your mind and learning to think with his mind. It means surrender-ing your eyes and learning to see through his eyes (just as Job sur-rendered his and saw the cosmos through the eyes of God). It means seeing one another and especially the destitute and displaced and despised in exactly the way he saw them: as himself, at once human and divine, with no distinction.

CHAPTER 9

THE WHIRLWIND PRINCIPLE

Here's a surprising but true fact: There are creationists more extreme than Ken Ham.

They seem to be mostly Catholics. The group's ringleader is one Robert Sungenis. Like Ham, Sungenis professes to take the Bible literally. Also like Ham, he clothes his indefensible ideas in the armor of scientific language. But his theorizing is truly, staggeringly retrogressive: He insists the Earth does not move. For him our fair planet sits motionless in the middle of all things. The other planets, the sun, and, one supposes, every star and every galaxy (not to mention something very major called *dark matter*), all move around us.

It is an audacious suggestion. While Ham wants to go back to 1858, the year before Darwin published the *Origin of Species*, Sungenis rewinds the calendar clear back to 1300. The medieval cosmos, widely considered to have taken its last breath sometime in the late seventeenth century, lives again in the hearts and minds of a twenty-first-century Catholic splinter group.

Sungenis and his collaborators have been pushing their Earth-does-not-move agenda through books, speaking engagements, and online for several years now, but in 2014 they took the next logical step and produced a documentary film. It's called *The Principle*.

The name of the movie refers to the key idea they reject: the Copernican Principle—actually, an assumption. It states that the Earth is not in a central, specially favored position in the cosmos. It may be extended directly to the Sun and to the Milky Way. A strong form of the Copernican Principle, called the Cosmological Principle, says that not only is the Earth not in a special place in the cosmos, but that there *are* no special places in the cosmos. What we see in our cosmic neighborhood is more or less what we'd see if we were anywhere else.

How do we know the Copernican Principle is true? Strictly speaking, we don't. What we *do* know, however, is how fruitful it is. If you make an assumption and subsequently get tangled in a thicket of problems and inconsistencies, you will eventually work your way around to questioning the assumption. But if the assumption leads to solutions and powerful, self-consistent theories, the scientific community tends to think it's true. And so far the Copernican Principle, in both forms mentioned, has been fruitful.

There is one form, however, in which it has not been fruitful. That is what you might call its temporal form. We've previously met Fred Hoyle, one of the Big Bang theory's detractors. Hoyle's own cosmic model, known as the Steady-State theory, assumed that there are no special places in the cosmos, and also no special *times*. In this application of the Copernican Principle, the cosmos has always looked more or less like it does today, and it always will. But this assumption, held by virtually all scientists until the late 1920s, was soundly rejected because it's inconsistent with observations. So while we cannot know with certainty if our assumptions are true, we do have ways of investigating them: good ones bear fruit and bad ones do not.

One of the reasons Sungenis and his group dislike the Copernican Principle is that they understand it to mean that because the Earth is not in a special place, then *human beings* are not a special species. "The world has been shaped by two great assertions—one places us in the center of it all and the other one relegates us to utter insignificance," writes Rick DeLano, the writer and producer of *The Principle*, on the film's website.[1]

But the Copernican Principle says nothing of the kind. It's not a principle about the relative significance or specialness of creatures, human or otherwise.

Far from Decent Society

We could, however, propose such a principle. And, in keeping with the convention of naming ideas after those that first popularized them, we could call it "The Whirlwind Principle." This principle may be stated: *The human species is not a central, specially favored species in the cosmos.*

It's tempting to reject this principle outright, for it suggests unsettling lines of thought. It slings mud in the face of virtually all Western religion and philosophy. It goes too far.

But then, so does the book of Job.

Job's journey, you will recall, began on a sunny day atop the human social pyramid. His significance not only surpassed all others in Uz, as a human being he was above every creature on earth. He was righteous, generous, fair-minded, wise, respected by all. He was the very reflection of the God who sat enthroned high above heaven and earth.

Or so he thought.

His descent took him first from the pinnacle of human society to its cellar: "But now they make sport of me, those who are younger

---

1. www.theprinciplemovie.com/principle-rocky-mountain-pictures-distribute
-highly-anticipated-documentary-theatrically-north-america-film-set-open-chicago
-october-24/.

than I, whose fathers I would have disdained to set with the dogs of my flock," he laments in 30:1. From the bottom everything looked different, and it was from this location that, over the course of thirty-six chapters, he argued with his friends over the meaning of wisdom, the elusiveness of justice, and the character of God. He thought he could go no lower: "My spirit is broken, my days are extinct, the grave is ready for me" (17:1).

But the whirlwind showed up and drove poor Job even further from the good things of life, further from decent society, further from justice, further from security. The direction was outward, away from human civilization and into the howling waste, the desolation of sand and rock, the empty and unmapped lands, and into the presence of chaos itself.

What he found out there, surprisingly, was life. True, it was not life as he normally thought about it. It was alien and strange, even freakish. It was wild and free. It mocked human civilization and refused human control. Some of it was modest, nearly invisible. Some of it was unthinking and violent. Some was primordial and fearless. It was not "pretty." But it was life, thriving in places and conditions we could never hope to survive, far beyond the comforts of human cities.

And God, you will remember, was delighted by all of it.

Like scientists with their Copernican Principle, before his descent Job carried with him a working, if unnamed, assumption about the centrality of human beings, a kind of inverted Whirlwind Principle. This faulty assumption was challenged by traveling to extremes and going beyond them, by being shown what could not normally be seen. The whirlwind took Job on a tour that was, in its day, cosmic in the full sense of the word. One can never be sure, but I like to think that if Job were written today, it's not to the desert that the whirlwind would take him, but somewhere far greater in scale and strangeness.

The Face of Our Wilderness

My night walks had become habitual. They were not solitary as a rule, but they usually turned out that way. A sophomore at Young Harris College, I was walking alone up an unlit mountain road in North Georgia. It was a little foolish, actually, for muscle cars were a source of fascination for some of the local young men. They relished furious nighttime flights up and down the sinuous mountain asphalt.

No place had been provided for a fool to walk. Almost without exception there was a wall of rock on one side and a steep drop-off on the other. In the silence of the night I could hear the cars coming a full minute before they roared past me, so I had time to press myself against a rock or crouch at the lip of earth's descent. As they passed I had to shut my eyes against the loss of night vision. It is unlikely that my presence ever registered with the drivers at all. If it did, it must have been as a ghostly apparition at the instant of passing.

Foolish it was, but peril is a vague thing in the mind of a young person, and I was drawn by a prospect seen only after sunset and in outposts of sweet remoteness: the night sky.

I walked in complete darkness. Other than the asphalt under my feet, the only way to tell I was on track was by looking up—stars shining between the trees created a kind of overhead reflection of the road, making it easy to follow.

Finally the road leveled and the sky opened to the north. I left the asphalt and walked freely across a field, miraculously flat and more than 100 yards on a side. I lowered my eyes as I went. I would not look up until I had walked a certain distance because I wanted an open view from the start. When I reached my destination I stopped and lay on my back upon the face of the planet with my feet pointed south. Then I looked up.

By that time I had taken several astronomy classes, so I had some idea of what I was looking at. Jupiter and Mars stood near the western horizon. Jupiter was bright white, and Mars was ruddy and darker. These occupied the extreme foreground. Light years beyond them, stars were scattered from horizon to horizon and outward beyond the edge of visibility, like the lights of ships spread across an infinite sea. Familiar constellations popped out one by one. The Milky Way was a glowing band arcing high above, farther out than the stars. I was also aware of a much vaster emptiness beyond the Milky Way, stretching beyond the limits of imagination and thinly populated in all directions by galaxies far too faint to see.

The face of *our* wilderness is heartbreakingly beautiful.

Earlier that semester our astronomy professor had told us something weird: of all the millions of catalogued stars, the only one known to host planets was the Sun. Now this is a simple thought, but I had never thought it. The idea of planets orbiting other stars had never even occurred to me. At the time astronomers suspected there to be many millions of planets out there, but this was only a conjecture.

Most people think of planets in pretty simple terms, possibly due to schoolroom space posters. Some of these suggest that our bright blue Earth is a member of a family of distinct personalities. The image is pleasurable and easily retained: colorful marbles rolling about the Sun on smooth curves. But planets are not personalities or marbles—they are *worlds*. They are complex and evolving. Just consider the two I saw that evening. On Mars there are volcanoes that dwarf Mount Everest, gorges that dwarf the Grand Canyon, polar caps composed of ice and solid carbon dioxide, dust storms, and seasons. Jupiter boasts hurricanes and auroras and sixty-seven moons, four of which are approximately the size of Earth's moon. Two of these are highly active, with volcanoes and ice geysers going off regularly. The geology and meteorology of the solar system is fascinating.

But our truest interest in planets beyond the Solar System (known as *extrasolar planets*, or *exoplanets*) is not geology or climate exactly. It's ET. Life is the point. So far as we understand things, which admittedly is not very far, planets (or their moons) are required for life. Only on such bodies can the conditions for life be met. Where there are other planets, there may be other creatures.

So as I lay there, wondering at the vastness and beauty of the wilderness overhead, I thought: *What am I looking at?* Who's out there? Are we alone? Is there some alien creature lying on some remote planet we've never seen, gazing out in Earth's direction, wondering the same thing?

Introducing Kepler-452b

The Whirlwind Principle suggests *yes*. If it's correct, then we not only share our planet with a spectacular host of God's creatures, we also share the cosmos with God's ETs. For this to be true, though, there have to be plenty of exoplanets out there.

As it turns out, there are.

As I write, news is coming in from NASA that a new planet, Kepler-452b, has been discovered orbiting a star 1,400 light years away in the constellation Cygnus. This in itself is not too big a deal, because the discovery of exoplanets has become a common occurrence. The first one was discovered in 1992, five years after my night walk, and they have been rolling in faster and faster ever since. As of today (July 2015), there are 1,593 confirmed exoplanets and 3,751 unconfirmed candidates. All of these, including Kepler-452b, are nearby (yes, 1,400 light years is nearby). But among them Kepler-452b is special. To understand why, you need to know a little about exoplanets in general and something called the "Goldilocks zone" in particular.

Like planets in our own Solar System, exoplanets come in all sizes, compositions, and orbits. Some are larger than Jupiter and some are nearly as small as the Moon. Some are made of gas, some of rock, some of ice. Some orbit close to their star and some orbit far away. Others travel on extremely elliptical orbits and still others on nearly circular ones. Not all combinations of these properties are conducive to life. For example, for a planet to support life, we believe that liquid water is necessary. Without water a planet will be barren.

The Goldilocks zone is a region surrounding a star within which water can exist as a liquid. Put the planet too close to the star and its water boils. Put the planet too far from the star and its water freezes. Between the boiling and freezing zones is the Goldilocks zone (not too hot, not too cold . . .). In this temperate region, officially called the *habitable zone*, water can flow and life can potentially exist. It turns out that Earth orbits near the center of the Sun's Goldilocks zone. Mars is also within it but sits close to its outer edge.[2] What we really want are planets within this zone. ET, we believe, can exist nowhere else.

So that's where NASA has been looking. The administration funds an extensive astrobiology research program. In its 2008 Roadmap, this program states the following as its first goal:

> Understand the nature and distribution of habitable environments in the universe. Determine the potential for habitable planets beyond the Solar System, and characterize those that are observable.[3]

The news about Kepler-452b is so big because it's the most promising data point, outside the Solar System, in the "distribution of habitable environments" in the cosmos—it's the planet most like our own. Its parent star, Kepler-452, is quite similar to the Sun. The planet sits well within the Goldilocks zone, is approximately the size of the Earth, and is in all probability rocky (like the Earth). Its year is about 385 days, just slightly longer than ours.

---

2. On September 28, 2015, NASA announced that it had discovered water flowing on the surface of Mars.

3. astrobiology.nasa.gov/media/medialibrary/2013/09/AB_roadmap_2008.pdf.

So today, when it comes to exoplanets that may host life, Kepler-452b is Exhibit A. It stands as one out of 1,593. There are certainly many millions more out there as good or better. It was Douglas Adams who, in his *Hitchhiker's Guide to the Galaxy*, wrote in all truth, "Space is big. You just won't believe how vastly, hugely, mind-bogglingly big it is. I mean, you may think it's a long way down the road to the chemist's, but that's just peanuts to space."[4] Big it is—so big that, if we hold to the Copernican Principle and assume that these local stars are not particularly favored with planets, we can project this number out to billions of Earth-like planets in the Milky Way galaxy alone, not to mention the whole of the cosmos.

Which is good news for the Whirlwind Principle.

Fresh Universes from the Cosmic Kitchen

There's more good news. Besides being liberally sprinkled with planets, our cosmos is strangely suited for life.

Suppose you get your hands on what I like to call the cosmic cookbook. In the cookbook are recipes for making universes. There are lots of them in there and you're free to make any one you like. You could make a cosmos with lots of black holes, or you could make one with no black holes. You could make one in which atoms never form, or you can make one in which only really heavy atoms exist. You could make a cosmos that would last forever or one that would collapse back on itself in a millisecond. You could make one in which stars consume their fuel slowly or quickly. You could make one in which stars don't form at all. You could make one that is flat or shaped like a sphere or a saddle or a donut. You could make one with two dimensions, or three or four or thirteen. You could also make one that is compatible with life, or not.

---

4. Douglas Adams, *The Hitchhiker's Guide to the Galaxy* (New York: Random House, 1979), 77.

Two things make the cosmic cookbook different from cookbooks you have in your kitchen. The first is that it contains not hundreds, but hundreds of *billions* of recipes (or more).

The second is that, instead of ingredients, its recipes require numbers—but only six.[5] Conveniently, the oven in the cosmic kitchen has six dials, one for each number. The recipes in the cosmic cookbook are very simple, consisting only of the numbers these dials must read in order to produce your cosmos of choice. You have many choices. On one page, for example, you will find the six numbers for a five-dimensional saddle-shaped cosmos with tons of black holes and no life. All you have to do is dial up the numbers on that page and press BAKE and *poof*, there you have it. On another page you'll find the settings for a cosmos that will last exactly twenty-three seconds. On another you'll find a seventeen-dimensional donut cosmos (a personal favorite). And on another you'll find ours, a three-dimensional flat cosmos in which stars burn slowly and life is possible.

Here's the clip-and-save point: there are *amazingly few* recipes in the cosmic cookbook in which life is permitted. The overwhelming (and by this I mean *totally-way-overwhelming*) majority of recipes produce barren universes. There are many conditions for a cosmos to be compatible with life, it turns out, and nearly zero recipes meet all of them. Many are barren because in them, planets cannot maintain stable orbits around their host stars. Others are barren because they do not last long enough for life to evolve. Others, because the chemicals required for life never form. Other universes are barren because stars never form, or because they do form but their temperatures never stabilize, or because they burn through their fuel too quickly.

All six numbers have to be *just right*.

For example, one number, called *epsilon*, measures the rate at which stars convert hydrogen into helium. This number happens to

---

5. I am using the numbers presented by Martin Rees in his excellent book *Just Six Numbers* (New York: Basic, 2000).

have the value 0.007.[6] If it were as low as 0.006 then there would be no helium or carbon or oxygen in the cosmos; if it were as high as 0.008 then no hydrogen would remain and water could not exist. In neither case would we be here to talk about it.

All six numbers are fixed within similar bounds. The fact that all six lie within their necessary-for-life ranges is surprising. Actually, *surprising* is an understatement. To get a sense of the probability involved, consider this picture. You are standing fifteen feet from a wall. On the wall are drawn, in random locations, six small squares. Each one is a half-inch on a side. You are given six darts and are blindfolded. You are then pointed toward the wall and told to throw all six darts in one heave. Imagine your surprise when you remove your blindfold to find one dart in each of the six tiny boxes. That is the kind of surprise I'm talking about. The numbers are perfect.

Now there is a certain sense in which this is unremarkable: *of course* the numbers are right. If even one of them fell outside its "box" we would not be here to notice it. But others see the fine-tuning of these numbers as a highly significant fact. They draw a different wall-oriented analogy: that of a firing squad. Suppose you are put up against a wall and a dozen people shoot at you with rifles from close range. After the roar of gunshots fades, you are shocked to find yourself still alive, untouched by a single bullet. On one hand you could say: Well of course they missed me—if they hadn't I wouldn't be here to realize it. On the other, as you lie in bed on the first night of your new life, you will wonder, deep down, why you're not dead. Something must have happened back there at the wall. Perhaps, in the immortal words of *Pulp Fiction*'s Jules Winnfield, "God got involved."

---

6. For the science-heads among you, this is the fraction of mass that is lost to energy in a reaction that fuses four hydrogen nuclei into a single helium nucleus, as determined by $E=mc^2$. This reaction occurs in all stars for about 90 percent of their lifetimes and is the current source of the Sun's energy.

The Cosmos That Knew We Were Coming

It's easy to see divine intention in these six numbers, as if God entered the cosmic kitchen and twiddled the oven dials with great care so the cosmos would be just right for life, for *us*. Others reject this notion on scientific grounds ("God did it" does not play well in scientific work). Some scientists interpret our six numbers to mean that there are many zillions of universes out there. These universes comprise something called the *multiverse*. This multiverse contains not just many but *all possible universes*. Each one has a different set of numbers, and we find ourselves in one of the few that support life because that's the only kind we *can* inhabit. It's like buying all the lottery tickets: you're guaranteed to win. As entertaining and ripe for science fiction as this idea is, however, it lies outside the bounds of science as I understand it. I just can't take it seriously.

My own problem with this particular idea of divine intention—God as cosmic chef—is theological. God is not a knob-twiddler of any variety. Such a deity seems too much like the God of classical theism. That God belongs to a cosmos I do not inhabit. That God belongs to the old cosmos, a cosmos in which ET—a nonhuman, corporeal, intelligent being—was not even a possibility. That God sits high above that cosmos and is distinct from it and has absolute control over it. That God is the Great Twiddler, standing outside all things and working the cosmos like a casserole. God doesn't work that way.

Yet I am unable to ignore this fact: the cosmos is narrowly fit for life but didn't have to be. The firing squad analogy carries weight with me. As Churchill said, "Nothing in life is so exhilarating as to be shot at without result," and I am both exhilarated and grateful when I look out at the cosmos and think of those six numbers. It makes me feel as Freeman Dyson might have felt when he wrote, "As we look out into the Universe and identify the many accidents of physics and astronomy that have worked together to our benefit, it almost seems as if the Universe in some sense must have known that we were coming."[7]

Only us? The Whirlwind Principle, when placed alongside other lessons from Job, says *no*.

I've already suggested a model of creation as gradual, continuous, and open-ended. In this view God is essentially creative and works cooperatively with the cosmos as it stands, continually drawing out the possibilities inherent in its chaotic raw material. This is done always with the participation of creatures and is never opposed to creation as it stands. This model not only resonates with a universe in which both structure and creatures emerge slowly, but it suggests that God is always creating across the cosmos and not just locally.

If this model of creation is correct, if billions of habitable planets exist in a cosmos well tuned for life and, in keeping with the Whirlwind Principle, we are not a central or specially favored species in the cosmos, the answer must be: We are not alone. There are others out there. Probably many of them. There is an awful lot of *out there* out there.

So Where Is Everybody?

There is one complication, and it is obvious: We have zero positive evidence for extraterrestrial life. The sky has been silent for as long as we've been listening. Why?

To tell the truth, in my optimism, I've ignored some problems. There may be *many* more requirements for life than six numbers and the presence of a rocky planet in the Goldilocks zone. It may be that a planet must also have the right location in the right kind of galaxy. It may be that its orbit must be nearly circular and stable

---

7. As quoted in John D. Barrow and Frank J. Tipler, *The Anthropic Cosmological Principle* (Oxford: Clarendon, 1986), 318.

over billions of years. It must also, we suspect, exhibit plate tectonics to stimulate biological diversity. A significant magnetic field should probably be present to protect its surface from radiation. And perhaps any habitable planet must be part of a system like ours, with small rocky planets orbiting within the paths of massive giants like Jupiter and Saturn. Our single, unusually large moon has helped to stabilize Earth's axis and thus its climate. Such a satellite might also be required. There are more possible restrictions and, taken together, they are severe. Truly habitable planets might be *extraordinarily* rare. Earth might be the only one in the Milky Way, or even in the observable cosmos. We and our fellow Earth-dwelling creatures might, in fact, be it.[8]

There is also this. If some extraterrestrial civilization within the Milky Way is even several million years ahead of us evolution-wise, and if they, like us, have a powerful inclination toward empire-building, they could have colonized the galaxy by now. It would have taken a few million years to do it, but that's a pretty short span in evolutionary time. A simple consideration of this kind led Enrico Fermi, one of the great physicists of the twentieth century, to ask: If life is so common in the cosmos, "Where is everybody?"

There are possible answers. Perhaps the creatures are more developed than us but are not interested in cosmic conquest. Perhaps they are just as developed as us but the time required for light to travel between stars is so great that we haven't heard from them yet. Perhaps there is plenty of life but it is not as developed as we are—it may be modest, like grass in the desert.

So yes, one can offer explanations for the lack of evidence for ET. Even so, the silence gets louder every day.

---

8. Of course there might be planets out there that harbor only simple life like bacteria and algae. It may be that not all of these factors are required in those cases.

Turning the Telescope Around

The jury is still out on the Whirlwind Principle. It's not clear whether it bears fruit or not. On the one hand we have a theology that views God as essentially creative and a cosmos that is strangely fit for life. On the other hand ET continues to elude us.

In the face of this nonconclusion I offer a confession. As optimistic as I am, and as suggestive as Job is, I cannot help but sense a note of desperation in our quest for extraterrestrial intelligence. I think it's a symptom of profound loneliness coupled with the collapse of traditional religion. But human beings cannot avoid religion altogether, so we listen. Night after night we search the cosmos, waiting and hoping and listening and looking. With our telescopes we gaze outward across billions of light years to the very edge of the Big Bang, desperate to find out where we came from, who we are, where we're going, and whether or not we are alone. We find Kepler-452b and the Internet lights up. And we do all of this for the same reason we pray and sing and worship: We are a bewildered species and we seek a connection to someone or something, visible or invisible. So perhaps the connection is *out there*. There's no scientific project more obviously religious than the search for extraterrestrial intelligence.

In the end, however, this outward search is guaranteed to bring us back home. Let's perform a thought experiment. Let's place ourselves on Kepler-452b and turn those same telescopes around and observe us observing the universe. What a strange, strange sight: Aliens! Extraterrestrial intelligence! ETs that pray. ETs that tell the truth and tell lies. ETs with fads, personality disorders, musical talents, and political ambitions. ETs that play games, build things, watch game shows, and chatter incessantly about themselves. What a discovery!

It is, to my knowledge, by far the strangest view in the cosmos. And whether the ETs are here or there, well, that's neither here nor there.

CHAPTER 10

COMING HOME

When I was a kid I was a member of the YMCA Indian Guides, which was basically Cub Scouts with headdresses and fringe. Like Cub Scouts, we Indian Guides often went camping. At some point in the late 70s, Dad and I left the city in our Pontiac Catalina, crossed the Georgia piedmont, and entered the low country. It was my first visit to the Okefenokee Swamp.

The Okefenokee covers nearly a half million acres in the southeastern corner of Georgia. In the nineteenth century, decades after the last of the Seminole had been driven out, the Suwanee Canal Company purchased the land from the state with the intention of draining it, for there was money to be made in selling the peat-rich acreage to rice, sugar cane, and cotton growers. Great canals, many miles long, were scored into the soft bottomland. But even the mighty will of commerce could not force the Okefenokee to relinquish its slow-moving tea-colored water, and after admitting failure the company looked in the only direction it had left—upward, at the towering cypress—and began logging operations. This ceased in 1927. In 1936 the swamp was declared a national wildlife refuge and was left to heal. Today it is home to countless species of birds, most visibly the tall waders—egret, heron, ibis, bittern—and various species of red-crested woodpecker. The Florida black bear is abundant, as is the swamp's most famous resident, the American alligator.

We joined up with the other boys and fathers and piled into canoes. After a two-mile paddle we landed on a low plateau abutting the canal. We fished for warmouth perch and bluegill as evening fell and, after eating and joking around a smoky fire, we bedded down. Dad and I lay side by side, completely still, listening to the songs of a dozen species of frog, and watched the turning sky. Sometime later, once the chorus frogs, green tree frogs, pig frogs, carpenter frogs, and all other local members of the order *Anura* had fallen silent, we slept.

Two hours after sunrise we put back in and drifted up the canal toward the car and home. Each canoe carried one father-son pair. As we traveled our canoe drifted to the rear of the convoy. I grew anxious as we fell behind the others. I began to lean harder into my strokes. Then I noticed: Dad was not paddling.

He said, "Don't worry, son. Let them go. Let's look around."

"But they're almost—"

"It's not important. There's no hurry. Let's look around."

Within a few seconds I relaxed. We rowed and we looked. After some time we rounded a bend and came face-to-face with a young buck, his head raised from drinking, his muzzle dripping. His antlers were mere buds. His head turned slowly, following us as we drifted past, and then he turned and disappeared quietly into the woods. That made me happy.

Gradually the great wealth of the place occurred to me. The Okefenokee hummed with animal life, but I was also struck by its living silences: Spanish moss and cypress trees and lily pads. We left the canal and paddled out into the prairie. The sky opened, a great shining ocean full of winged life. The water shone brassy and clean, and my happiness turned to joy. I was overwhelmed by the wonder of the place. I nearly cried. There is no explaining it.

Back on the canal we continued our survey, quietly noting the nuthatches and dragonflies. Then Dad brought the canoe to rest, his eyes set on the bank behind me. The water was motionless beneath us. In a low voice he said, "Son, I'm looking at the biggest alligator I have ever seen. On the bank. Turn around slowly."

I thought quickly. Dad had spent a number of months as a young man running heavy cable by hand across the swamps of Louisiana, where he had seen lots of big snakes. He had told us stories. Surely he had seen alligators also. But maybe not. Figuring further, I knew that he had at least been to Atlanta's zoo, which contained, as far as I was concerned, at least one plenty-big alligator. I turned, conjuring Godzilla.

And there it was, sunning itself, eyes closed, the long side of its body along the bank, no part of the alligator more than a few feet from the water. It seemed large, especially when it dawned on me that this was not the zoo. Nothing stood between us and the alligator, a wholly wild creature. Its kind was known to have shredded and devoured virtually all other species in the swamp, including deer and bears. It was the Okefenokee's apex predator.

"Let's go take a look," Dad said.

I didn't want to, but what's a boy to say to his father? We paddled up close, parallel to the animal. As we moved the swamp seemed to hush. Once we got near enough we saw that the beast was longer than our canoe. There was no more than a foot between the boat and the bank, and the alligator only a short foot beyond that. In silence we paused to regard the creature's details.

But the only detail that registered with us was its tail, and that directly, for the reptile jerked awake and plunged through the narrow opening between bank and canoe, its tail slapping the hull with enough force to nearly capsize us. As I tried to find my balance I caught sight of the animal passing beneath us like a great shadow. It moved with surprising speed. We were left clutching the gunwales and staring into each other's faces, our breath held close, the canoe rocking like a cradle.

When we reached the Catalina I was exhausted. I lay beside Dad on the car's front bench seat and slept hard as we drove north toward the city. I dreamed I saw the young buck lapping water on the canal bank. Periodically he raised his head and stood still before returning to the drink. Then he began struggling mightily, digging his hooves into the earth, shaking his head side-to-side. He was trying to free himself from the alligator's jaws, which had somehow become clamped to his muzzle. The reptile was in the water and pulled down hard on the buck. No blood flowed yet the predator's oversized teeth were entirely red, as if carefully painted. Somehow the deer held his position but sank further and further into the soil. The alligator pulled the deer straight down. Eventually the soil closed neatly like water over the buck's head and the animals were gone.

I woke to the sound of heavy Atlanta traffic, tired and hungry but happy to be home.

The Fifth Dentist Knuckles Under

Job's cosmic tour is over. The vortex has taken him places few have been, shown him things few have seen, taught him things few know. He has been forever changed by the earth and sky and a host of oddball creatures thriving far from human civilization. Nothing has been missed: everything from the modest desert grass to the raging Leviathan has conspired to open his eyes. The cosmos has shown him that tradition can sometimes be corrected by experience. It has demonstrated that God is not a wise man in the sky who sees things more or less like Job himself does. God's admiration for marginal creatures and cosmic chaos has been made clear. And, on top of all this, Job has found divine favor. God has praised his borderline blasphemy and condemned his friends for clinging to traditional wisdom in the face of clear counter-evidence.

Thus enlightened and vindicated, he heaves himself off the ash heap, brushes off, prays for his friends, and sets off for home.

Then, unbelievably, our Fifth Dentist knuckles under: "The Lord restored the fortunes of Job when he had prayed for his friends; and the Lord gave Job twice as much as he had before. The Lord blessed the latter days of Job more than his beginning . . . he had seven sons and three daughters" (42:10, 12-13). This dramatic reversal of theme destabilizes our conclusions: Job has, in the end, been rewarded for his righteousness, and in the most obvious of ways. Perhaps tradition trumps experience after all. Apparently the model of God as supreme patriarch is more robust than we thought. And maybe God is in fact primarily interested in rewarding and punishing human behavior.

I've already expressed my personal distaste for this turn of events (and my pet theory explaining it). These revised conclusions are hard to shake, and it may not be possible in the end to do so. I don't know. Yet I would like to offer another way of thinking about it, a way that saves—and even underlines—our conclusions.

Wood and Water

For better or worse I tend to be a purist. I like my coffee black and my wine red. I also like to keep my religious traditions separate. Nevertheless, when I think of Job's strange denouement I am unavoidably drawn to a proverb that comes out of Zen Buddhism: "Before enlightenment: chop wood, carry water. After enlightenment: chop wood, carry water." I understand this to mean two things. First, enlightened or not, you must do the work that's in front of you. Second, enlightenment does not necessarily change everything you do. Its effects are real but are not always conspicuous.

The word *enlightenment* is not biblical. It basically means awakening (and might be roughly translated into the Christian term *revelation*). In the West it has accrued all kinds of New-Agey resonances and has been used to mean everything from "finding your inner self" to "becoming one with the universe." But, to borrow a phrase coined by my high school social studies teacher, I believe enlightenment is less hippy-dippy-yippy than that. It is about seeing the world as it is and doing things with intention and presence of mind. Followers of Zen might say that, whatever an enlightened person is doing, they are doing *that*. The enlightened mind is not distracted. While chopping wood, there is only the wood. While carrying water, there is only the water.[1]

Before enlightenment, wood was chopped and water was carried. But there were other things going on. In some cases you might have done these things while thinking you'd rather be doing something else. In others you might have done these things poorly. Maybe you did them well, but with an eye toward impressing someone with how much wood you chopped or how deftly you carried the water. On some days you chopped wood or carried water with an anxious heart, worried about the coming winter or the drying well. Or—to stretch the imagination a little—perhaps chopping wood and carrying water were the top jobs and you did them with an attitude of entitlement or smug satisfaction. In no case is there only the wood. In no case is there only the water. There is the wood and water, yes, but there is also "in addition to."

This sounds like someone we know. Before his day of calamity and his cosmic tour, Job performed the top jobs—administering justice and caring for the poor—admirably. No judgments were wiser and no care was more helpful. But while judging he had something in

---

1. There are Christian writers who have written on themes that seem to come quite close to what Buddhists call *bodhi*, or enlightenment. They value simplicity and purity of intention and insist on living deliberately and with no distractions. A medieval example is Meister Eckhart, a fourteenth-century Dominican friar who championed "detachment" above all other Christian virtues, even love, and a modern example is Simone Weil, who wrote about the supreme value of what she called "paying attention." In extolling these virtues these writers represent a quasi-Eastern current in the stream of Christian thought.

mind in addition to his judgment. While caring there was something in his heart in addition to the good of the other. Before his losses and his tour of the cosmos, Job administered and cared while nursing a well-concealed admiration of his own excellence. He administered and cared with the assumption that those he judged and cared for really were different from him. He believed that administering justice and caring for the poor were especially lofty jobs and that doing them so well made him a lot like God.

His wood-chopping and water-carrying were distorted by the "in addition to's" of narrow traditionalism, self-satisfaction, and a well-cultivated God complex. Looking back on the good old days from atop his ash heap he cries, "When I went out to the gate of the city, when I took my seat in the square, the young men saw me and withdrew, and the aged rose up and stood" (29:7-8). He relished his kingly—god-like?—status in the eyes of those whom he helped: "I smiled on them when they had no confidence; and the light of my countenance they did not extinguish. I chose their way, and sat as chief, and I lived like a king among the troops, like one who comforts mourners" (29:24-25). In an earlier passage Job challenges God to judge him and, in so doing, betrays the fact that he sees God as a large version of himself. Presuming that the Lord would be as thoughtful as himself in judgment, he says, "I would speak to the Almighty, and I desire to argue my case with God. . . . I have indeed prepared my case; I know that I shall be vindicated" (13:3, 18).

Logs on the Ash Heap

Jesus spoke in humorous terms about those who are distracted by "in addition to," asking, "Why do you see the speck in your neighbor's eye, but do not notice the log in your own eye?" (Matthew 7:3). In Job's story, loss and the cosmos conspired to remove several logs from Job's eye.

The first is traditionalism. Tradition itself is not the enemy, for it can help us see things we would otherwise never see. But it may also prevent us from seeing things that are right in front of us. In his telescope Galileo clearly saw four tiny "stars" following Jupiter across the sky and he quickly recognized them for what they were: satellites of the great planet. His colleagues in the academy, however, refused to admit that Jupiter could have moons.[2] Their traditional understanding of the heavens did not allow for such things. Tradition distorted their vision.

Moreover, established ways of seeing things always favor someone, and in this case it was Galileo's detractors. They had more at stake than whether or not Jupiter had satellites—they had their careers to think about. At the time university education was based almost entirely on Aristotle, and if the great philosopher was wrong their whole system of thought—and their livelihoods—might be at risk. They got their own selves mixed up in it. That was the cost of their traditionalism; that was the log, the "in addition to" that prevented them from seeing the obvious. Their self-interest prevented them from seeing the moons of Jupiter.

Galileo was not distracted. His vision was not clouded by fear and insecurity. When looking through the telescope, he saw the view through the telescope. Like Job who spoke of God what was right as he argued with his friends, Galileo's eyes were log-free.

Job also left the log of specialness on the ash heap, not in the sense of uniqueness but in the sense of being separate from and superior to the general run of creatures both human and otherwise. The self-perceived favorite child is always obsessed with status—think

---

2. Opposition came from within the church too, but that was a rather complex affair and developed slowly over decades. Galileo's most committed enemies, especially in the years immediately following his telescopic discoveries, were academicians who held no real power and who were therefore keenly threatened by Galileo's science.

of the older brother's reaction to the prodigal's coming-home party (Luke 15:28-30)—and the fear of losing it. Job was no different. Chapter 31 is full of Job's claims of moral excellence: he has not been false; he has not been enticed by strange women; he has not ignored the complaints of his servants; he has not withheld from the poor; he has not trusted in his wealth; he has not rejoiced at the downfall of others. Given all this, God, who sees all and who is just, must therefore treat him favorably. "Does [God] not see my ways, and number all my steps?" he asks (31:1, 4). Justice demands that the good boy be rewarded.

But suffering and the cosmos show Job that, despite his excellent moral sense, he is not so special. Just like everyone else, he's at risk of falling to the bottom of the social order. Moreover, God shows Job that he not only has no cause to consider himself above other people, he has no cause to consider himself above other *creatures*. The wild ass, the ostrich, the vulture, Behemoth and Leviathan—these too have a share in the great love of God. Job, finding himself to be one small creature in a cosmos full of them, is able to sit still and let the log called specialness be extracted from his eye. Once gone, he sees the truth: "I am of small account" (40:4).

Such a perspective soothes many anxieties. Last year our youngest went through a period during which she grew worried as she lay in bed at night. She would fret about monsters, or "invisible people," or her homework assignments. On a few occasions she became terribly fearful and self-conscious. She loves animals, so I suggested she think about them—not just animals in the abstract but individual kinds: foxes, bees, rabbits, birds, one after the other. And I suggested she picture them in their dens and hives and holes and nests, bedding down and sleeping. "All the animals are going to bed just like you," I said. "Think of their closed eyes, their breath, their little bodies. They're in our backyard and far away, right now, falling asleep." It worked.

It worked for Job, too. The fears are different—fear of failing one's homework is not the same as the fear of not being the best—but the self-obsession driving them is the same. The world came into focus for both of them when they stopped thinking about themselves and started thinking about something bigger, something cosmic.

Unchecked, the idea that you're especially distinguished can grow to the point that God is cast in the image of the creature. Severe distortions of vision can occur when this happens. Perhaps the greatest of these is that the creature comes to believe that they really know something about God. Job, who, pre-calamity, thought of God as a magnified version of himself, certainly thought he had God figured out. That's why he struggled so mightily with his losses: he himself would never allow such an injustice in Uz.

On the Surface, a Bubble

Thanks to God and the cosmos, when Job comes home he leaves these logs on the ash heap. Without anything "in addition to," he is free to chop wood and carry water. That is, he is free to do what he had done before—administer justice and help others—only now without distraction. Now there is only justice. Now there are only the poor.

None of this is in the text, of course, which says nothing about Job's civic activities post-ash heap. But that silence is precisely why I suspect that he returned to his previous station as judge and caretaker of Uz. Such wealth—twice what he had before, which itself was more than anyone else—would bring with it great influence, and it's easy to imagine that he ended up doing again what he had always done so well. We all must do the work God gives us, and all worthwhile work is ennobling, be it chopping wood and carrying water or administering justice and caring for the weak and marginalized.

We may therefore translate the Zen proverb: Before revelation: judge wisely, care for the poor. After revelation: judge wisely, care for the poor.

If we were to watch him post-crisis, we would see him doing many things he had done before: sit at the city gate, administer justice, hear cases, support the downtrodden of Uz, go home and have dinner with his new family, which is a lot like the old one: wife, seven sons, three daughters.

But the sons and daughters are different this time and so we may, if we watch him closely, see the old man remember his losses in private and mourn them, perhaps in prayer. But the text gives us none of that.

The text does give us *something*, however. Job's vision is no longer blocked by presumptions and fears so at times he doesn't always do things the way things are supposed to be done. He's no longer playing by the same rules as everyone else, so the concerns that distract others—fear of being different, a desire to be thought extraordinary, presumptions about God—are no longer worthy of consideration.

This makes sense of why, two verses before closing out the story, the author slips in the names of Job's three daughters (the sons go unnamed) and bothers to tell us that "their father gave them an inheritance along with their brothers" (42:15). The practice of giving daughters an inheritance is attested to elsewhere in the Bible, but only in the context of a family with no sons (Numbers 27:1-11). So this is a small but unorthodox move on the part of Job, fully consistent with a man who is no longer concerned with social niceties.

I love the subtlety of it. It reminds me of a scene in *Finding Nemo* in which a hundred underwater mines explode at once and all that is seen on the surface is a single bubble, a small but undeniable expression of deep drama, an easy-to-miss sign that nonetheless demands an explanation.

God via Flamingo

After coming home from the Okefenokee and resting up I did pretty much the same things I did before I went: I went to school, I played with friends, I went to church, I did Indian Guide stuff with Dad. But something had changed. Like Job's daughters' inheritance, the difference was small but unmistakable and, in a way, unorthodox: I began noticing the birds in our backyard. They were newly interesting to me. My interest quickly grew into a near-fixation. My parents encouraged me, buying field guides and recordings of bird calls. I came to know all the species around my house by sight and most by song. I learned about far-off and rare kinds I would never see except in books. In private I mourned bygone species: the passenger pigeon, the ivory-billed woodpecker, the great auk. Straining for realism, I drew pictures of birds. John James Audubon's *Birds of America* became my favorite book.

Much later, on a clear day early in my junior year of college, I was passing through the entrance hall of the library and my forward momentum was gently arrested by the fabulous S-curve of Audubon's *American Flamingo*. A full-sized facsimile of the great book was on display in the lobby, opened to its most famous plate. As I stood still looking down at that otherworldly beast, I remembered my own miniature copy of *Birds*, borrowed from the DeKalb County library years before. Details of its images came back to me: the strangely large heads of the screech owls; the tail of the sedge wren, held at an obtuse angle to the bird's body; the semitransparent water through which one could see the large black feet of the trumpeter swan. I wanted to reach through the glass and look long at every outsized page.

At the time I had rejected Christianity for its shallowness and irrelevance. The cosmos had become far more interesting to me—indeed, a *painting of a flamingo* had become far more interesting to me—than any church or religious organization or anything at all that went by the name "Christian."

But God called to me through Audubon's flamingo just as surely as God called to Job through the deer and the hawk and the ostrich. I didn't know it at the time, but as I stood there I heard the distant roar of the whirlwind—an echo of my day in the swamp.

I now know that, through that crazy bird, I was being called toward a faith I could not have even imagined. But right there in the Bible I had taken to church as a boy every Sunday, in the Bible that I had studied in high school and even in college, hiding between the books of Esther and Psalms, was a story with the power to change my life. Job celebrates those on the cosmic margins while pointing us beyond traditionalism, beyond anthropocentrism, toward a confounding and essentially mysterious God who is nevertheless known to water the desert grass, admire the constellations, feed the lion, laugh at the ostrich, channel Leviathan's might, and, most miraculously for us human creatures, show up, time and time again, at the ash heap.